First published in Great Britian Growbag Publishing, 2020

Growbag Publishing
Bury Green Farm House
Old Park Ride
Waltham Cross
Hertfordshire
EN7 5HY

Print version ISBN: 9798663092074

THE ESTATE AGENCY REVOLUTION

Making your business **VITAL** through your **DATA**

Mark Burgess

www.iceberg-digital.co.uk

THE ESTATE AGENCY REVOLUTION

About the Author

Mark Burgess is the CEO of Iceberg Digital, a multi-award winning software company for Estate and Letting agents. He is a best-selling business book author and is asked to speak regularly at both National and International events. In 2019, Mark was asked to host a TV show on Sky called 'Raising Your Game', where he would Interview other successful entrepreneurs to give hints, tips and hacks to businesses around the world.

Mark has been featured on Forbes.com as one of the entrepreneurs in the world making a difference, has been a judge at the Business Book Awards, and has been nominated for a lifetime achievement award for his work in the Prop-tech industry.

THE ESTATE AGENCY REVOLUTION

Acknowledgements

Everything that I achieve in life is thanks to the amazing people around me. Writing my second book has been a bigger challenge than the first book, but it has been made possible by the constant encouragement that I receive from my stunning wife, Hayley, and my slightly mental children, Fraser and Grace. I hope one day they will be old enough to read this book and feel even just a tiny bit as proud of me as I am of them.

I would also like to take this chance to thank all of my incredible team at Iceberg Digital, for allowing me the time away from the running of the business to complete this book. You are all amazing.

Finally, I would like to thank any of the clients that work with me or Iceberg Digital, for putting your faith into what we do and allowing us to try and make a difference in the way our beloved industry works.

THE ESTATE AGENCY REVOLUTION

Kind Words

As this book has been written specifically for Estate Agents or Realtors. I thought it might be nice to hear from a handful of actual Estate Agents that I have helped over the years in order for you, the reader, to have confidence that the work I do actually makes a real difference to the people in our industry...

"Technology is leading most of the changes around us and we don't ever want to miss the opportunities that come with it. Thankfully, with Mark's outlook and forward thinking approach, the Estate Agency industry doesn't have to be left behind, enabling agents like us who want to be different, to continue to set themselves apart from the rest. We look forward to seeing what else he has got up his sleeves..."

Pippa Scott | COO | Sandersons UK

"Mark will make sure that you remember that it is YOU who is your USP, he reminds you what excites you about the business, strips away what's holding you back. Then he encourages you to put yourself back together but only better, more efficient and empowered. Then you are fit for purpose in the new and exciting world of agency as you've never done it before."

Jacqui Bradshaw | Manager | Jacksons Estate Agents

"Agents work in the same way that they always have, yet over the last decade the industry has changed beyond recognition. The Estate Agency Revolution/Mark Burgess shows how much has changed, and what you need to do for your business to thrive. I'm so glad to be a part of the revolution I know that my business is already using data for its growth in the future!"

Kelly Jeffrie | Managing Director | Love Property

"Mark has been like a beacon of light within the Estate Agency industry and I am so happy to have met him 12 months ago when I started my journey with Iceberg Digital. What this man doesn't know isn't worth knowing and he has really opened my eyes to the change that is needed within our industry. I would describe mark as a 'saviour' and industry guru. Thank god he picked estate agents to save."

Louise Young | Owner | LL Estates

"I have been in the Estate Agency business for 30 years. I met Mark Burgess about two years ago after reading his first book. I was immediately blown away by his refreshing down to earth approach and immediately started to use Iceberg Digital. It was a massive success and with his guidance and mentorship he has helped to transform my agency for the better We are now looking at the bigger picture, big data and how to successfully nurture customers on a journey to success."

Damien Cooke | Owner | Cooke & Co

"I first met Mark at a strategy session for a system we were already using but didn't really know why. I found the session eye opening and Mark's presentation style engaging in an unusual way! I have been in touch with Mark regularly since and he is always happy to engage, offer his thoughts and help wherever possible. A friend to our industry...."

Steve Neocleous | Director | Mishon Mackay

"Meeting Mark Burgess in the last 2 years, has not only opened up my mind to understanding the true future and value of data, processes and systems but he has inspired me to unlock my true purpose in life as an individual. A life changing person to meet."

Rob Brady | Innovationist | Iceberg Digital

"I have been in touch with Mark for almost 2 years and became a client of his approximately 9 months ago. Mark's enthusiasm for the industry and seeing his clients succeed is wonderful to experience. It is obviously infectious as the same could be said for all of his staff. As I write this we are just returning to work following the COVID-19 pandemic, Mark's communication with me has been exceptional, he has been like another business partner. Bouncing ideas around with us, providing webinars, guest speakers, pushing us to evolve our business. He doesn't have to do this - I am already a paying customer, I already have his products and for the majority of companies that is where it stops.

"He always seems to be ahead of everyone else. The support is simply incredible, and I haven't experienced that from any other person/company in this or any other industry. EVER"

David Long | Director | Newboulds

"Mark is a revolutionary genius, years ahead in his industry. Mark has personally had a huge influence on me and my approach to business and countless others. Mark's unique vision is undoubtedly shaping the future of the property industry."

Andrew Sharpe | Director | Sure Sales & Lettings

THE ESTATE AGENCY REVOLUTION

Contents List

Introduction

The Good News and The Bad News

NOTE: THIS BOOK WAS WRITTEN BEFORE AND DURING THE CORONAVIRUS CO19 PANDEMIC AND THE EFFECTS ON BUSINESS THROUGHOUT THE WORLD WERE YET TO BE SEEN. AS SUCH ANY REFERENCES I HAVE MADE TO BUSINESSES & TURNOVER ETC MAY HAVE CHANGED.

THE ESTATE AGENCY REVOLUTION

The good news, if you are an Estate Agent or Realtor, is that this book was written for you. The bad news, if you are an Estate Agent or Realtor, is that you won't have a business in a few years.

In this book I will explain in simple terms why that is and also how you can stop that certain end happening to your business. I just ask one thing of you in return - you must finish the whole book.

On my travels I often get asked how I ended up doing what I do. It has been an interesting journey. At school I was not what you might call a model student. I was always in the top sets, but I was a constant cause of frustration to my teachers, who regularly would tell my parents that I was capable of so much more. This was true as I can honestly never remember doing any form of homework or revision, but somehow managed to just do enough, or maybe show enough promise, to always remain in these top sets.

When I hit 14 or 15, my relaxed attitude seemed to turn more into one of disruption. Not in the sense that I would cause disruption to my teachers or to my mum, I was always a reasonable person, but more in the sense of starting to believe I knew best.

I am sure this is almost universal in all teenagers, but mine led to me literally breaking out of all of the normal unwritten or written rules of society. I would never go to school, only occasionally popping in to take part in some of the sports lessons, but again, I was not like the sort of unruly teenager you might be picturing. I just could not see any future in putting my efforts into something that was not really leading anywhere and I was happy to have that reasonable conversation with anyone who cared to have it.

The problem was that the person on the other end of that conversation was usually not quite as reasonable, in the sense that their argument always seemed to be based around 'you just have to'. Anyone that knows me will know that is a sure-fire way NOT to get me to do something. With my immediate built in response to be - I don't HAVE to do anything.

Once I left school I did not have any idea of what I wanted to do. I knew all the things I did not want to do, for instance work for a big corporation in an office, or a government building etc. I knew that would not be good for me due to the rule following issues.

Weirdly, at 16, I enrolled into college, thinking that it might be different as it was a subject I had chosen for myself, but it was no different. Another on and off year took me to 18.

I wanted to do something different, but as most kids find out as they begin to enter the adult world, what you want to do and what you need to do are two very different things and the need soon outweighs the want in terms of your mum shouting at you to just get a damn job and contribute!

I had a few dead end jobs, the type where a friend's parent puts you in touch with someone who then gives you a job as a favour on some silly below minimum wage income. You know the type - where they don't really need you and you don't really want to be there.

Then at 20 I stumbled into Estate Agency. I loved it.

A young Mark Burgess starts
his first job in Estate Agency.

There were no rules, other than 'come to work', which I could just about manage. After that, you were given targets and left to figure it out for yourself. I could do it my way and ultimately live or die by that. Of course, you have a manger and regional directors, etc., who try to train you and give you pointers, etc., but ultimately you are judged on your figures.

This was like a breath of fresh air for me as I had always submitted my work and achieved pass grades to the tests and exams I had been asked to do, but still the teachers were unhappy with me, as I had hardly attended any of their lessons. I could not figure out the problem with this. In Estate Agency, I was free to do what I wanted, within reason. Provided I was top lister and top seller, no one cared – again, within reason.

I did well in Estate Agency, but the pay was awful. I was working and living in the poorest borough of East London, which is really not much more than a slum. The daily routine was dealing with young people who could not afford to live anywhere else and property developers trying to pull some sort of trick on you.

Working in this market gave me great insight into how making money from property worked, so I decided to become qualified as a mortgage advisor in order to learn the ins and outs of how I would start to build a property portfolio without having any money, and that is what I did for the next 10 years.

I remained employed for a few of those years, having a stint in the City in IT recruitment (my second love is computing), before starting my first business in 2001.

From there, I built up a great property portfolio and several businesses until the financial crash in 2007/8.

The crash of 2007/8 pretty much wiped out everything I had built up. I lost almost every property or was forced to sell them and my business at the time was owed over £100,000 in unpaid bills by companies that all went into administration, sending my business down too. It was a disaster and I was back to the needs over wants situation where I was now being told to just go get a job!

On top of the rubble left from my now destroyed empire was my last £20,000. I asked my wife if I could use that in order to try and rebuild and she agreed.

In 2009, I started Iceberg Digital with the purpose of creating great content for Estate Agents and helping them to distribute it, as I could see that content marketing was the way to go.

Iceberg Digital was about building a lifestyle business. Something that could get us back to the life we wanted to lead, and it did that! There was no grand plan, there was no purpose. We created great products and sold them to Estate Agents and again we rode that wave for 7 good years. It was fun.

In 2016 this changed. Another financial storm, not as bad as 2007/8 but this time over Brexit. 2007 was still reasonably fresh in the minds of the agents that had been through it and so the uncertainty over Brexit lead to them cutting everything back, just in case. Our revenue dropped by 50-60% almost

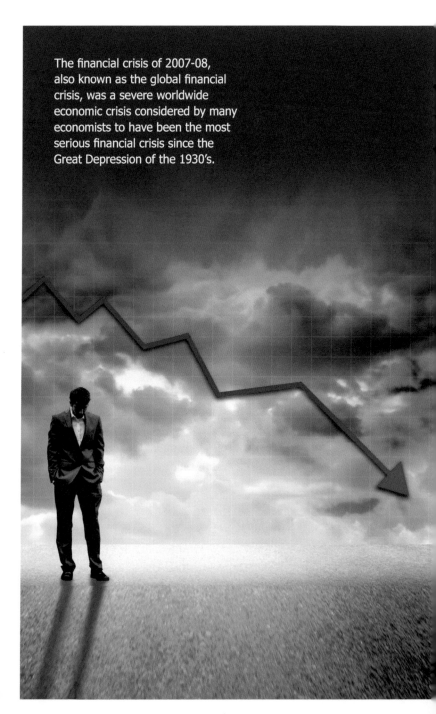

The financial crisis of 2007-08, also known as the global financial crisis, was a severe worldwide economic crisis considered by many economists to have been the most serious financial crisis since the Great Depression of the 1930's.

overnight and I started to wonder how you step off this roller coaster of ups and downs in business?

I began to look more into the science of business, as opposed to just thinking about how I could make some money, such as what are the common traits of very successful long-lasting businesses? I began to go to more networking meetings and found some incredible mentors who had all built and sold multi-million-pound businesses.

I also started to look further into the data behind my business.

Since somewhere around 2011, I started to get heavily into marketing automation and how that could work to improve productivity. We had used many off-the-shelf systems, but had invested in building our own one, as my thinking had moved beyond what was currently available and internally we were having phenomenal success using our own system, which we had named Fragra.

Now that many of our processes were running through Fragra, I was starting to think more about how that data could be tracked in order to make forecasts, in much the same way that the weather forecast works or even the economic forecasts. For instance, surely there must be a correlation between the amount of money we spend on marketing, the number of visitors we get to our website, how many new clients we take on and how much that client spends with us. If I could start to figure this out, I would know how much we make for every £1 we spend.

As it turns out, I was not the first person to think of this and it is a generally accepted formula if you are working in a corporate business that is being run by people that DID go to school, and university!

This is known as LTV vs CAC – Life Time Value (of a customer) versus Customer Acquisition Cost. I won't start going into detail, but every business should know this and if you search it on Google you'll find lots of information around it.

However, when I would look at the formulas, they all seemed so weak and, because they could not really get the full data, they would take approximate numbers out of the balance sheet and base things on numbers they could see, such as how many enquiries vs how many sign ups, etc.

Because I had not learnt this in a classroom and had only thought about how it should work myself before discovering it, I was not bound by these imaginary rules or formulas. I would think - hmmm, there is a better way of doing this but to do it I'd need a way to track data such as who visits my website; how many times; from which source; and then eventually tie that to who spends money on what, etc; over what period of time; and after how many chasing emails?

From here I began to walk into the world of Big Data and eventually onto Machine Learning. Of course, to me they were not called Big Data and Machine Learning, as I never studied what I do. Instead, I invented my own system.

Now I am not by any stretch of the imagination claiming

that I was the first person in the world to invent Big Data or Machine Learning. What I am saying is that there are many people around the world who push the boundaries of what is possible in their field, because they are not completing tasks laid out for them from a text book, but instead are making it up from their own thoughts on how they can improve the industry or the world - Innovators.

Innovators are people who have no prior knowledge of something but dream it up anyway, as opposed to implementers, who are equally as valuable but who implement other people's ideas extremely well. I have come to know these two types of people as Visionaries and Integrators, which I will cover later in the book.

It may be that a version of the Innovator's dream already exists, but there are minor differences because it came from their own mind, and not a 'how to guide'. Those minor differences, I have come to realise, are the ones that make people say, WOW.

I have won many awards, spoken both nationally and internationally, had my own TV show on Sky, had a best-selling book and advised countless companies on their strategy. I do that because I love innovation and I love the idea of talking about something that I love and seeing the same lightbulbs go off over the top of people's heads as I do. I have also discovered that a passion of mine is sticking up for the underdog.

Currently, I am on a mission with Iceberg Digital to revolutionise industries. We are concentrating that effort on Estate Agency, due to my passion for that specific industry and the fact that currently, it is a huge underdog in terms of being able to survive against the flow of technological advancements. We aim to change this by helping the existing industry to evolve instead of waiting for a technology giant to come and eat them up. We plan to do this firstly in the UK and eventually around the globe, to give this industry the type of technology, data and algorithms that will actually make a significant difference to the way in which they work and the experience their clients receive.

Once we have achieved this in Estate Agency, we will look for a new industry to revolutionise. But for now, and for the purpose of this book, I will be focusing on Estate Agency.

And that is how I ended up doing what I do.

Chapter 1

It is hard being an Estate Agent, but are you making it harder?

In 2017 I released my first book called 'Where Did My Industry Go?' The book was around the concepts of how marketing in today's world works for Estate Agents, or Real Estate Agents, as the rest of the world calls them.

Although that book went on to become an Amazon best-seller in 4 different categories, I made a school boy error in creating that book, which I would only learn after the event.

The error was that I had assumed (big mistake) that the computerised systems Estate and Letting Agents used had evolved since the days when I had been a critic, reviewing those systems for some of the biggest industry trade publications some 12 years earlier, back in 2005. They had not!

As a result, I was contacted by Estate Agents (and other types of businesses) from all over the world, saying how insightful they had found my book and asking my advice on which systems they should use to do this!

Initially this was not a problem as I am also the CEO of a company called Iceberg Digital, which produces software for that industry around better productivity and marketing, BUT what I had not bargained on was the problem of the existing tech in that industry being so far behind on such a universal scale.

The systems that Estate Agents were using were still the exact same systems that I had been reviewing back in 2005 and as we know, a whole lot of things have changed in the world since 2005. Just to put it into perspective, in 2005 there was no such thing as an iPhone. Nokia and Motorola were the world's most popular mobile phones.

The Nokia 1110 was the most popular phone in the world in 2005) Motorola blazed the trail for thin phones with a clam shell form factor, while Nokia had started releasing the first of its phones to have access to the Internet. In 2005, Facebook was not even open to the general public, and was still called 'The Facebook'. In 2005 no one had heard of or knew how life changing Google Maps was going to be as this was its launch year.

Even Gmail had only just begun. Your DVD collection was still constantly growing, stores like Blockbuster were still alive and kicking and Internet videos were barely a force to be reckoned with. Before 2005, there was no such thing as YouTube and Netflix did not even start their streaming service until 2007.

Now, 15 years later, the world is a very different place. In fact, if you were a child in 2005, let's say 10 years old, then you would now be 25 and not really know a world without all of these advancements - you would laugh at the Nokia 1110 as if it was from 100 years ago, not just a decade and a half.

Now we have a world where the phone function of your 'phone' is a secondary feature, for many maybe even an optional feature! Google Maps is ingrained into our societies. Can you even imagine getting a map book out to look up directions? How would you find local restaurants? Directions for walking or driving to places? Facebook and all of the companies they own, i.e. WhatsApp, Instagram, Messenger, Oculus and Facebook itself, surround our every day lives. Netflix is the go-to TV channel for an ever growing percentage of people, so much so that it currently consumes 15% of the entire world's internet bandwidth from people watching TV shows and movies on their platform. That is without YouTube, which has become the definitive resource for knowledge, how to guides, and the new form of kids TV - which is kids watching other kids shout and play video games. Who even knew there could be such a thing?!

It truly is a different world, literally. Not even a slightly similar one. But still after all of this, Estate Agents are using the exact same tech as they were in 2005 and much of it was not even new then. If you are one of them, then think of it in the same way as still forcing your team to use paper maps! It is not about just using tech for the sake of it. It is a productivity and customer experience issue.

Tech is not the answer to all of the problems currently facing Estate Agency, or any business, but it is one HUGE problem that needs to be overcome. In the world we currently live in, you can't operate in a way that will be efficient for your company and your customers, using tools that were built so long ago for a completely different world.

We have spoken about the huge changes technology has brought in the past 15 years but just stop for a moment to think about the tiny improvements that have come into our everyday way of working through technology that would still be making your life a misery if you were using old tech.

For instance, imagine as an Estate or Letting Agent, taking 15 photos of a property and then having to upload those photos one by one to your system. That is how systems were built back then, and imagine how much time just having a batch upload would save that company, even if they are only taking on 10 properties a month, let alone if they are taking on 100! I mean, I can send 15 photos to someone through WhatsApp in a few minutes, maybe even seconds, so why should it take me 15 minutes to do it at work?

Imagine continuing to go out on 20 valuations every month and then having to put those people into a 1-31 system or a callback diary and hoping to keep in touch with all of them forever manually, like that is even possible. The alternative is to have systems that will keep you at the top of their thoughts at all times through email and social marketing, then give you instant alerts when they are active and it is the right time to touch base with them, any of them, FOREVER.

Think of all the forms you have to fill out manually and how time consuming that is. The same questions that you ask different people over and over again about their buying or selling circumstances and then manually entering that data into your software.

How much more effective and productive it would be if those people could complete those questions themselves, online, at any time of the day or night. You would then have the information sucked into your systems and thus present the opportunities to the right people in the organisation to follow up, along with automated marketing around those opportunities.

Imagine just having a big database of Buyers, Tenants, Landlords and Vendors just sitting there doing nothing, as opposed to an intelligent system that finds them all in Facebook and constantly communicates with them through email and social, and alerts your team as to who are the best people are to call for new viewings, valuations or instructions. How much more productive would your team be?

All of the old ways of working may seem like the norm because you have done it that way for so long, but just stop for a moment and you will realise that it really isn't the norm to work that way anymore. There are so many more examples of this, which I am sure you can think of in your own business. Changing the way you are forced to work could save literally tens or even hundreds of thousands of pounds a year in productivity costs if they were improved, aside from the increase in sales. The buyers that register with you are used to services that deliver to them exactly what they are looking for and even suggest other things they might like. Systems from 2005 barely even allow you to send them properties that fit their correct criteria, let alone start to learn what else they might like by tracking what they look at on your website and what other similar buyers also view.

Currently, most Estate and Letting Agents are not even working in the right age. Not because they don't want to, but because the system they are using is holding them back, leaving them fighting with one hand permanently tied behind their backs. In fact, it is more like they are fighting with both hands tied behind their backs and both feet tied. The only reason they are currently able to cope with that is because most of their opponents, i.e the other agents, are in the same disposition, which keeps it an even fight.

As more and more agents start to use the new breed of software, it will be like stepping into the ring with a young and fit Mike Tyson. It is not even going to be a competition, it will be a blood bath. Agents investing in these new ways of working are not willing to settle for old tech anymore and they are on the rise. Maybe there is one in your area already, maybe not, but it is coming through now and this book will help you prepare for the huge change sweeping through our industry.

I know from the 1000s of Agents I speak to worldwide, that many are concerned over whether they will be able to adjust to using newer tech, but let me reassure you, if you do worry about this, don't! You know why? Because you have already moved on technically in every other aspect of your life. You already do have a smartphone in place of a 2005 Nokia. You already do use Google Maps. You already do use the internet, Amazon and Google and so on. You already know what is a good customer experience in today's world and what is not. It is now time for you to give your Estate and Letting Agency a big shake and say, "It is the 2020s!"

We need to wake up before the knockout punch lands - Mr. Tyson has started his ring walk.

My first book created a platform for me as I began to be regularly asked to speak at business events both in the UK and Overseas. This led to me eventually being approached by one of the TV Channels on SKY to have my own TV show called 'Raising Your Game', which draws out hints, tips and hacks for entrepreneurs via short interviews with amazing business people.

Mark Burgess
speaking at
Estate Agency X 6

I have since been featured on Forbes.com as one of the entrepreneurs in the world making a difference and was nominated for a lifetime achievement award for my work in the Proptech industry.

But this journey has been one of deep education and reform around some of the fundamental ways in which businesses that are having big wins going into the 2020s use the data to do so. Also, why without this knowledge of how to take action, other types of business will follow the long line of companies before them that have been superseded by those that do work in this way.

As it turns out, from my years of real world research, this game of win or lose is not so much a chance occurrence, but actually quite predictable.

These are the reasons that have led me to write this book. This book is not so much about the 'how' but more about the 'why' of something you will come to know as Big Data Lifecycle systems and the machine learning that they can create.

By definition, Big Data is an evolving term that describes any voluminous amount of structured, semi-structured, and unstructured data that has the potential to be mined for information. In other words, Big Data helps us to extrapolate valuable conclusions out of massive volumes of seemingly unrelated information.

Lifecycle systems are software applications that are not focused on a specific part of a potential or current customer's journey with your business, but instead, are looking at, well, the whole Lifecycle and ways in which to make your business more productive and work smarter.

For the past 20 years these types of systems have been exclusive to global corporations. The likes of Amazon, Apple, Google and Facebook. In fact, many would argue that they invented them. Yet the principles of how this kind of autonomous marketing through data works and how a business can actually build an algorithm unique to them, is now available to any size business, and the best part? You do not have to be a super geek to do it! In the same way that people around the world used to have to study maps to navigate from A to B, but now just let the computer do it for them, these systems will just 'do it for you'. However, you do have to be willing to want to use the computer as opposed to the map and combine the power of tech with humans.

But this 'Big Data' idea is just one more advancement of technology, right? Then why is this so important?

In this book I will clarify it, so that by the end of the book, you will see that this is the biggest shift in the way businesses work since the industrial revolution. Furthermore, that if you don't start to implement this new way of working and understand the principles of it within the next 2 years, then over the course of the next decade, your business will go the same way as the horse and cart, and will happen to you at the speed of light as businesses around you are adopting this way of working.

Throughout this book I will share my message with you

through real life examples that are in 'everyday' terms, allowing you to understand the principal difference between what you might have been told or even sold by someone else, and why they would have done that. Allowing you to see a clear path for your own business to implement the simple changes needed to thrive in the 2020s.

My goal for those of you that read this book to completion is that it is the catalyst, the light bulb moment that, no matter your age, or the age of your business, suddenly allows you to see what is actually happening in the world around you. In my head I see this as the moment that Neo is offered the red or the blue pill in the film 'The Matrix'. You can take the blue pill, and close this book now, close your eyes to the tidal wave coming your way and just continue along until it hits, or you can take the red pill and complete this book to suddenly awaken and see the 'real world' around you. But an important thing is that if you want to do that YOU MUST FINISH THE WHOLE BOOK, you may even end up referring back to it or reading it more than once.

Reading part of the book, feeling like you get it and moving on will not be good enough, so if you are that person, do yourself a big favour right now and commit to finishing the entire book. You will need it to refer back to sections when you are unsure of your path or how you make sense of the conflicting information that is purposely being thrown in your direction. There are reasons, which I will go into during the book, as to why certain companies don't want you to know this information, or take action on it. Take the red pill and finish the whole book, it might just change the course of your business life.

You can take the blue pill, and close this book now, close your eyes to the tidal wave coming your way and just continue along until it hits or, you can take the red pill and complete this book to suddenly awaken and see the 'real world' around you.

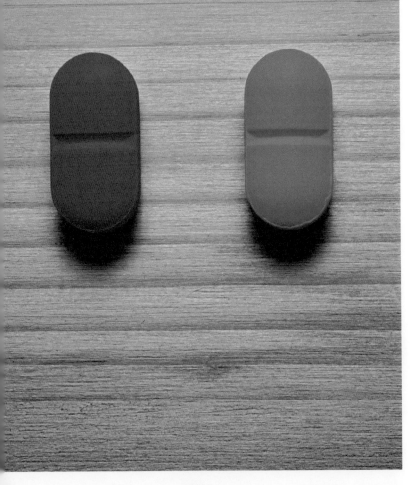

As I mentioned earlier, I have now spoken at countless conferences and seminars to thousands of people around the world about this subject and what has become perfectly clear to me is that there are usually two main things that hold a company or person back from implementing the change. The first seems to come from an ever so slight feeling of fear. The fear that the words 'Big Data' or 'Machine Learning' and similar terms, can strike into any individual. The feeling you get when you think you are now talking about something that you feel unqualified to talk about, but here is the thing, Big Data is nothing to be scared of.

You will never need to feel like you know and have mastered all of the possible things surrounding it, in the same way that you do not need to know how to plaster a wall in order to have a wall in your office plastered, or identify when it needed re-plastering. You do not need to know how to build a website in order to have one for your business, or know when it is out of date. It is only the why part that you need to know, and in this book I am going to give you that in a simple-to-understand way.

The second reason I usually see for procrastination around this subject, is that there are no immediate benefits. Yes, you read that right. There are no immediate benefits.

In much the same way that if you move from a paper based filing system to storing all of your files in a computer, there will be a benefit in doing that but not until all of your files have been transferred over. However, you still need to buy and implement the computer and the software BEFORE you can transfer the files. This does not mean that you should not invest in the computer. Building Big Data systems have immense benefits for businesses from a productivity perspective but they arrive once there is enough data to create the learnings.

Imagine if someone told you all of the benefits in life that your child would have should they learn to read and write and then go on to to gain a great high school education and a Degree in their chosen field, but because they could not have the Degree immediately you just didn't bother. Sounds absurd, right? But this is the choice 1000s of businesses are making when they ignore Big Data systems. The information those systems need is all running through your business anyway, you are just not tracking it in any meaningful sort of way because the pay off would not come tomorrow.

The thing is, when that pay off does come for a competitor business, your only option will be to try and solider on through life without the said benefits, or go right back to the beginning and start the process your competitor went through in order to get there. Just the same way that once you realise how helpful a degree might have been, you have no choice but to solider on without one or go back to school and start at the beginning.

In the following chapters of the book, I will describe how we have ended up in the situation we currently find ourselves in. How companies like Facebook, Google, Amazon and Apple, have managed to achieve more value in the last 20 years than some of the biggest companies in the world have done in the last 100 years by using Big Data, and how this is now possible for all levels of business - for the purpose of this book, specifically Estate and Letting Agencies.

If you are someone that wants to have an understanding of how all of this works but does not want to actually have to 'plaster the wall' yourself, this book will change your business life and quite possibly your personal life as well.

IT IS HARD BEING AN ESTATE AGENT, BUT ARE YOU MAKING IT HARDER?

Chapter 2

The history of the problem:
It's not personal

Although many species note the passing of time, only our own species is capable of sharing accounts or memories of past events and turning these into stories or "histories."

As humans discovered ever more precise ways of keeping track of time, they have also developed more accurate ways of keeping records and recording history.

But what exactly is history? I guess we could argue forever about that, but for the purpose of this book, let's just agree that it means "a shared knowledge of the past."

Why is it important to know about the past? How does that help us make better decisions in the future? If humans are the only species creating the stories of history, how do the other living creatures deal with this? For instance do animals, or even plants need history?

In fact, all living things carry "memories" of the past. Animals need to be able to keep track of the seasons so they know when to hibernate, when to hunt and when to have children. Many rodents and birds store nuts and other food in special hiding places and they need to remember where they stashed them so they can find them months later.

Even plants seem to record the passing of time. If you slice through a tree, particularly in a region with lots of seasonal changes, you'll see "growth rings." Every year a new layer grows just under the bark. There is often a light part formed early in the year and a darker part that forms later, so each ring represents one year of growth. Wet seasons typically produce thicker rings than dry seasons. So, dendochronologists — the scientists who study growth rings — can frequently figure out the exact year in which each layer was formed. They can also see evidence of climatic events such as droughts or forest fires.

However "tracking the past" isn't the same as having a "memory" of the past. A tree ring might record the date of a major fire, but the tree wouldn't respond if I asked, "Do you remember the great fire of 1730?"

Only humans can share their knowledge of the past, because only humans have a communication system powerful enough to share what they know and learn, but even the incredible human brain can only store a certain amount of information before it starts to forget things. Because of this, humans have come up with ever more sophisticated systems to store their data as a reference point.

From inscribing on the walls of a cave, right through to the storage of paper files in miles of cardboard boxes and then, eventually, placing all of that information into computer hard drives for both storage and the sharing of information on the internet.

But, if we rewind on that for a second, when we spoke about history and memories in terms of plants and animals, they only use that information for the fight or flight survival element of their existence. How could miles and miles of cardboard boxes, each filled with 1000s of individual files, possibly help humans with that particular problem, if you are not able to recall the data inside those boxes in order to make better decisions? And more importantly, if it does not help with that problem, what problem is it helping with?

Does the human brain instinctively know something we are not recognising? Why do we find it so hard to let go of old information? Of course, for legal purposes a record would need to be kept of certain transactions and such like, but as I type right now, why do I have old sheets of paper around me with random notes on that I do not want to throw away? I have no idea what is on those bits of paper. I will be very unlikely ever to go back to those bits of paper, but still, for some reason I am uncomfortable with the idea of just throwing them all away.... Why?

As mentioned at the start of this book, my business specialises in software for Estate Agents, so I will use that industry to base my examples on, but hopefully these examples will be good enough for you to translate the ideas to your own industry.

So, for a real world example, let's go back to when record keeping and the gathering of data in Estate Agency was paper based.

There were two main file types kept - one for properties, also containing the seller's information and one for buyers. At regular intervals, each member of staff would be forced by their manager to 'cleanse' their box of potential buyers by going through and literally ripping up and throwing away the details of any people that we felt were 'time wasters'.

What quite gave us the qualification to have this psychic ability to see into the future and decide if someone was a serious buyer or not, I am unsure, but we were asked to do it anyway.

For the property records, we would keep those files until the property was either sold or withdrawn from the market. Once the property was sold or withdrawn, the file would go into the archive, which basically means a box in the basement with a month and year written on the front. These boxes could not be kept forever as the space was limited, so to the best of my knowledge, after 5 years, the oldest records were destroyed. Then, around the late 90s to early 2000s, the future arrived into mainstream Estate Agency. Specific software for Estate Agents!

Bill Gates future of a computer on every desk had made its way into the Real Estate sector, generally accepted as one of the laggards of technological adoption. The dreams being created on these systems were what now seem like simple access databases, not dissimilar to excel, where you could store all of your information without the need for paper or cardboard boxes.

Now you could add buyers, sellers and properties to the computer. But what impact would this have?

Initially, the impact was great. As an agent, you would no longer have to 'cleanse' your list of buyers as you could just automatically match your potential buyers with all of the properties you had loaded onto the software. Press another

Around the late 90s to early 2000s, the future arrived into mainstream Estate Agency. Specific software for Estate Agents!

button and the software would email all of those buyers with the details of the matching property, albeit a very basic match based on a very general location, number of bedrooms and possibly a price. Easy.

Or so we thought at the time. As it turns out, a person's search for their ideal property involves many things that were beyond the limitations of software in the year 2000. After all the world had only just been introduced to the BlackBerry phone and the first iPhone was still some 7 years away.

As I mentioned, the property matching at the time was based around 3 things:

1. Is the property in the buyer's price range?
2. Does it have enough bedrooms?
3. Is it in the correct general location?

Whilst this is a logical way of working for a software developer, the actual factors that decide if a buyer likes a specific property boil more down to the look of the property, the condition of the property and the very specific location of the property, as two neighbouring roads can be extremely different.

This was all possible when we, as agents, were working from the memory of conversations that we had had with the buyers, but the introduction of this mass storage of information destroyed something that made Estate Agency fundamental to not only finding the right property, but to selling the property to the right person for the best price too. The personal touch of Estate Agency.

When I had my box of buyers, I knew them inside out. I never sent them random properties just because those properties were in the right general postcode. I knew they were looking for a specific estate.

I knew, when I valued a property, exactly who we had registered that was going to buy that property too and how much they could afford to pay for it.

The next stage of this depersonalisation came from the property portals. There were many over the years but currently the two main ones that remain are Rightmove and Zoopla. There are others but none currently worth mentioning for this purpose.

Whilst Zoopla did not exist back then, they did buy up most of the successful original portals, so for the ease of this explanation we will use them.

These portals again showed much initial promise to Estate and Letting Agencies. They arrived like a white knight to save the industry from the huge expense and short shelf life of the local newspapers and to be fair, they did do just that.

Unfortunately, they also created an extra layer of de-personalisation. They did this because Buyers could now sit at home and happily keep themselves informed of what was on the market and where. The property matching on the portals was not only more sophisticated than that of the Estate Agent's, but it covered all of the properties for sale, not just those on with that one agent.

This led to my buyer no longer needing to hear from me about properties, and instead of me, they would contact the agent if they saw something of interest.

The agents used these portals to tell sellers what a 'great reach' they could have and as such, could now not reverse out of using them.

Personalisation in Estate Agency was dead. This gave rise to commoditisation, in that all Estate Agents now seemed the same. They all had a 'Big Database of buyers', they all could 'List my property on the portals' and, as a result, any useful knowledge that could have been gained from our history and memories was no longer being retained in the process. It just became about who would charge the least.

This process was not instant, but took place over the first decade of the 2000s - from 2000 to 2010 roughly, but as I mentioned earlier, Estate Agency is a laggard when it comes to technology. This process had taken place in certain other industries as much as a decade earlier. In fact, outside of Estate Agency, the world had moved on dramatically from this concept, seen the problems it created and, by the end of the 2000s, had started to try and find the solutions using Big Data.

Since then, the shift in the way these types of companies work has been so significant over the past decade to 2020 that, according to the Harvard Business Review, people who have been in business for at least a decade should define their businesses as BBD and ABD, or Before Big Data and After Big Data.

You may be forgiven for asking whether 'Big Data' is not just an electronic version of the basement archive. If an Estate Agent has 32,000 contacts in their estate agency software, do they not already have Big Data? The wording could trick you into thinking so, but the answer to those questions is 'no'. So, what is Big Data and how is it so different that Harvard would consider it so ground breaking that they would mark an entire age by it?

In the mid-2000s, Internet and social media giants such as Google and Facebook began uncovering, collecting and analysing a new type of data. Whilst the term "big data" didn't enter the common language until around 2010, analysts recognised this new information was qualitatively different from the small data of the past and would help them to bring back the personalisation of a service on mass, without having to return to the paper based systems of the past.

Small data was generated by a company's internal operations and transactions, such as the current estate agency software, but this new data was externally sourced, drawn from the Internet, public data sources and third parties.

As more and more of people's everyday activities began to become trackable online by the evolution of online banking, social media, online publications and video streaming, so more and more data on an individual was being generated. But so what?

With the arrival of big data, new technologies and processes were developed at light speed to help companies turn data into insight and subsequently, profit. This allowed a new age of businesses such as Facebook, Google, Amazon, Apple, Uber and WhatsApp to go from start-up to superpower at astronomical speed.

Big data required new processing frameworks such as Hadoop and new databases such as NoSQL to store and manipulate it. These technologies were simply not available or possible back in the age of small data (BBD) and, as such, it would never be possible to convert a software system built BBD into a system that could work in this new way. In the same way as it would never be possible to build up a Spectrum 48k computer from 1982 into an iPhone, even though, technically, they are both computers.

The world moved on.

Except for Estate Agents.

But what has all this got to do with memories and history? Big data is an advancement in the way in which the software you are using can read and manipulate the outcomes. If you remember that the original Estate Agency softwares were built to match properties on 3 very rigid criteria of general location, price, and bedrooms, Big Data systems gather evidence by collecting previously unseen information to provide a very personalised user experience.

For instance, although we may have entered a contact into our system as looking for a 3 bedroom house, up to £500,000 in Chelsea, our Big Data system will pull in the information of which properties that person keeps looking at on our website and start to suggest that actually they are looking in a very specific part of Chelsea and have also looked at 4 bedroom properties up to £600,000. It may also have noticed that this particular buyer has looked at a property on our website 4 times but is yet to book a viewing on that property and as such, it will tell the email part of our system to contact them asking if they would like to view. It can also ensure that person will see that property again when they next log onto Facebook with a button for them to book a viewing and track to see if the email or the Facebook advert is more effective. Finally, it can alert the right member of our team internally that this person is someone they should call or follow up with in order to try and book them in for a viewing on that property. God, I wish I had that tool back in the 90s when I was an agent!

That is a very basic and simple example of how data that you are not responsible for entering into the system is being used to carry out automated functions, work smarter and always be in the right place at the right time for the right people. Revolutionary in-memory or in-database analytics are now being paired with responsive methods and machine learning to deliver real-time insight and results.

Predictive and prescriptive analytics, which give insight into the probability that an event will occur in the future and recommend possible courses of action, are now key tools for business executives and on-the-spot decision-making through the use of analytical apps.

Just as an animal records history for survival, we are now able to make real use of the data that flows through our business in order to deliver a micro personalised service to every single person, no matter the size of our contact data, and start to foresee events, both good and bad, that are likely to happen, in order to take actions that will speed them up or prevent them.

The personal touch in Estate Agency has returned. You can be not just useful again, but Vital!

THE ESTATE AGENCY REVOLUTION

Chapter 3

You're not currently building a vital business

Having the Data in order to make your marketing and your service personal is one thing. Actually making it work is quite another. For this you need to have software systems in place that have the ability, not only to create insights using the data, but also to learn from that data using machine learning. You must also, know the type of data you want to start with, to add into your learning in order to think up ways of getting it, as opposed to just randomly collecting any data and then thinking, "right, what shall we do with that lot?"

So for instance, if you need to know how long someone has lived in their property in order to see if there is a trend around that, then you can include that question in your market appraisal information gathering stage.

This may sound like things are about to get way too sci-fi for you, but actually you are surrounded by machine learning in your everyday life and in this chapter, I will try to break down some examples of this, in order for you to see just how important it is for your business to think about data and employ systems that will bring machine learning into your Estate Agency, or face the end of your business.

One of the issues that machine learning has brought into the world is that it has made some businesses vital and others, well, pretty un-vital. Let me explain further.

Traditionally these are some of the things that an estate agent might currently say to a potential seller in order to demonstrate why they should be using their service and why they are vital to them in that process:-

1. **What the agent might say:** They may talk about having a local 'network of offices' to give you super local coverage.

Problem: The problem is that this is really just a carry-over from a time before everything was done online and you could reach people on the other side of the world just by going on the internet and, therefore, isn't a particularly vital selling point to the client as to why they should use your agency.

2. **What the agent might say:** We can launch your property in style and standout from the crowd. We've teamed up with Rightmove, Zoopla and other property marketing specialists to bring you this perfect selling pack.

Problem: Rightmove, Zoopla, or any other property website doesn't make YOU vital, as any agent can use them. The rest of that paragraph is really just intangible noise.

3. **What the agent might say:** Professional photography

Problem: This idea is also a throwback. It is really not that long ago that to take a really good photo you needed a very expensive camera and some pretty expensive training – not to mention a powerful computer with editing software, to do a really good job. Although I am not sure how many agents advertising professional photography even went to those lengths.

In fact, it is not even that long ago that the photos needed to be developed.

Now the public are used to being able to take high resolution, quality images with their mobile phone and apply a filter in seconds. I am not suggesting that you should use a mobile to take your photos, but it is not something most sellers would see as something that they needed to pay you significant amounts of money for. It is a standard task when selling something these days, even if you are selling a second hand bike on eBay.

So, by all means talk about the importance of getting the photography right, but the idea that I NEED you because you can take professional looking photos? Nope.

The list of these 'non vital' reasons that a client should use you to sell or let their property could go on and on, from floorplans, to 360 virtual tours and everything in between. As we looked at in the previous chapter, estate agency software and the portals have commoditised Estate Agents. You have become a middleman, you have nothing of your own in all of those things that makes YOUR business so special.

This is why agents always come back to that old thing about people buy people.

They went with us because they liked us. That is nice but it is a very risky strategy and usually, when you really dig into it, not true. This is why so many businesses and even industries are going under, one day after the next.

Thomas Cook became a middleman, as I can book my holidays myself from my sofa. Blockbuster became a middleman, as I can order the same films from the comfort of my own home. Comet (electrical store) – middleman – I can order them online from anywhere. Staples – middleman – I can order stationary online or even get it from the supermarket. Phones4u – middleman – I can get a mobile phone from any mobile phone or technology shop, on or offline. Clinton Cards – middleman – not needed. Bathstore – middleman – not needed.

So how do businesses make themselves vital? They use machine learning on their Big Data systems in order to create algorithms with their data, which makes their business more productive and in turn helps the customer achieve their goals quicker. Once they have this, the client needs them, as only they have the algorithm.

So let's look at some examples for how companies use Big Data to become vital, when they could just be middlemen.

Google: There are 3.8 million searches made on Google every minute of the day, but Google is, on the face of it, just a middle man taking customers to the answers to their questions. Google feed that data into Big Data and machine learning systems. They have been doing that for over 20 years and because of this, Google knows you so well, that it can finish your sentences for you and bring you up the perfect results for all of the information stored on the internet in milliseconds, and importantly, ONLY Google can do this, as no one else has as much search traffic as Google in order to make a better algorithm than them.

Because of this, Google is vital to their clients (advertisers), as only Google can be as accurate as they are at putting the right ads in front of the right people.

Facebook: 2.45 billion users, 4.75 billion pieces of content shared daily and 510,000 comments every minute! Facebook run Big Data and machine learning systems to study all of the data that flows through their hands and, as a result, much like Google, Facebook is vital to their advertisers. Unlike Google, the Facebook users are not searching for products, but instead, Facebook is being used to highlight products to the right people who did not even know they needed that product or service. So, whilst Facebook could easily have been a middleman like all social media platforms before them, they have now created algorithms using their data that have made them vital to their clients (advertisers).

Netflix: 139 million paid subscribers, Netflix streams take 15% of the world's downstream bandwidth. Netflix users spend 1 billion hours watching movies weekly. The concept is all about being a middleman, i.e. Get content from TV shows and Movie makers and distribute it to consumers. However, Netflix have used their data to create algorithms that not only show them what certain people like to watch, but what else they would like to watch, based on their viewing history. No one can do what they have done without it taking years and years of Big data and analysis, as there are 90,000 hours of video being watched every minute on Netflix.

Because Netflix now knows what content people want, last year alone they spent $13 billion on content. FOX spent $200 billion, but the difference is, Netflix KNOW all of their shows are going to be hits and they market them for free to their audience. Fox are hoping some of their shows are hits and that the press pick up on them!

Whilst you might be thinking "Ok but they are all tech companies", this is not exclusive to tech businesses just because they are using tech to do it. So let's look at a more traditional business that has woken up to this idea and is implementing the change. For this I'd like to look at McDonalds.

McDonalds biggest acquisition in the last 20 years was in 2019 when they paid 300 million for Machine Learning business, Dynamic Yield. "We've never had an issue in this business with a lack of data," said McDonalds CEO Steve Easterbrook. "It's drawing the insight and the intelligence out of it is what we hadn't done and begun to connect the technology together".

So how and where will they use it?

McDonald's serves around 68 million customers every single day. The majority of those people never get out of their car and that's where McDonald's will deploy Dynamic Yield first. At their drive-thru restaurants. The digital displays that you currently see when you go through the drive through, automatically change, based on simple things, such as if it is the breakfast menu or the lunch menu, or special limited edition burgers, etc. The rest stays pretty static.

With Big Data and Machine Learning, Algorithms crunch

data as diverse as the weather, time of day, local traffic, nearby events, and of course historical sales data, not only at that specific franchise, but around the world, to show customers what other items have been popular at that location, prompting them with potential up-sells, depending on their order.

For instance, If someone orders two Happy Meals at 5 o'clock, that's probably a parent ordering for their kids on the rushed journey home from school, or an after schools club, so it will highlight a coffee or snack for them and they might decide to treat themselves too. If successful, it will do more of that. The system may go on to incorporate number plate recognition and bring up their last few orders to make a repeat order easy to do.

As with any machine-learning system, the real benefits will likely come from the unexpected. For example, if the drive-thru is moving slowly, the menu can dynamically switch to show items that are simpler to prepare, to help speed things up. Likewise, the display could highlight more complex sandwiches during a slower period.

Away from the drive through, their customers that download the mobile app could see their recent order come up on their phone as they walk up to the store.

All of these options will not just increase revenue, but make the customer experience not only better, but also easier and more enjoyable than any other fast food restaurant, making them more vital than their competitors.

A company that amasses as much data as McDonald's will find no shortage of algorithmic avenues. McDonald's CEO Eastwick said: "We're going to have real-time information, as we start to connect the kitchen and dots together, further back through our supply chain. "As you start to link the predictive nature of customer demand all the way through your stock levels in the restaurant and the kitchen, you can almost flex it back down through the supply chain."

One more example of a traditional business that has been around for many years and is using big data and machine learning to evolve and thrive is Coca-Cola.

Coca-Cola's chief big data officer said "Social media, mobile applications, cloud computing and e-commerce are combining to give companies like Coca-Cola an unprecedented tool set to change the way they approach I.T. Behind all this, big data gives you the intelligence to cap it all off."

One simple example of how they use this big data is inside their mix your own drink machines, where they study the most popular combinations and, because of that, have now launched Cherry Sprite.

Coca-Cola has used Big Data and AI in so many ways, as they have realised that if they do not take advantage while they have the data flowing through their business, the business will slowly drain away.

Now can you see how businesses are not just buying marketing software anymore, they are buying Big Data systems, so that the data that flows through their business can be in the right kind of systems to create algorithms to make themselves vital. These businesses don't really have to change too much, just adjust the systems they are putting the data through, and then only they have that particular algorithm.

The odds are being heavily stacked in favour of the companies that are building big data systems and new entrants to their market place can't possibly compete, without first having all of that data insight, and to get it, they would have needed to have been building a Big Data system for just as long as their competitors with the same or more levels of transactions.

You can also see why these companies will continue to grow and be vital and why companies without this will die or have already died. These businesses are making it almost impossible for anyone to catch them. Their value is actually not just in their revenue, but in the fact that if anyone wants that level of data, there is only one place to get it and that would be to buy the company. The price to buy that company will be whatever price they want to charge.

THE ESTATE AGENCY REVOLUTION

Chapter 4

APIs and the 'open' platform
– The devil in disguise...

I have set out how Big Data systems are not in any way the same as systems with big amounts of data, plus how you need all of your data in one place in order to allow for machine learning on that data. I would now like to try and clarify some of the ways in which business owners or companies take the wrong path with this, whilst actually trying to implement change, and how certain companies are purposely misleading you on this, and why.

In the last decade, a new breed of the world's most powerful companies have arrived, and each and every one of those companies use a big data system. Some of those companies have been going slightly longer than just the last decade, but their real growth has taken place in the last ten years, ABD (After Big Data). There are a couple of main reasons for this. The first is that Big Data as we see it today did not exist throughout their whole company's existence, and the second, is that Big Data takes time to start having an effect – there is no 'instant benefit' and this can often lead to companies abandoning their efforts before the effect has kicked in. I will cover that further later in this chapter.

Look at a company like General Electric. They are a monster of a company. They were founded in 1892 and, as I write this book (as the effects of the CO19 Coronavirus are still being taken into account), had a market cap valuation of £691 billion. They are a traditional business and quite rightly. It has taken them over 130 years to get that level of valuation.

Let's compare that to a company like Alphabet (Google). They were founded in 1998 and, at the same time as General

Electric, had a market cap valuation of £700 billion. In just 21 years, with most of that growth in the last 10!

Even a company like Apple that has been going since 1976, really just trundled along valuation wise until the mid 2000's when all of this started to change. Similarly, Apple had a valuation of £861 billion and regularly move in and out of the number one position as the most valuable company in the world.

The list of these overnight superpowers is getting longer by the day. Google, Facebook, Amazon, Apple, Uber, Tesla, Alibaba, WeChat, Tencent, the list goes on.

But for every new super power there are 1000 companies that have built products and services that existed before Big Data and they still need you to buy their products in order for them to turn a profit.

Because of this, the information and solutions given to businesses on how to be successful is somewhat grey to say the least. A mixture of misused terms and downright misleading information can quite easily lead a company down a wrong path.

The biggest culprit of this is the 'API or 'open system'. The typical pitch from a software provider that does this, goes something like this:- "We have an open market place and you can connect our system up to lots of different external systems in order to make your life easier."

The key thing here is that what is actually being said is that our system does not do the function you require, but we can send your contacts information to another system that will. Just remember that Big Data is not about 'just doing' things. Big Data is about pulling in data to your main central system from transactional and external sources, like the Internet, public data sources and third parties, so that your central Big Data system can learn from all of the information.

What is to be gained from sending your contacts' details to another system so that it can send an email? Nothing.

So whilst you might be performing a similar function, actually you are not competing with a company doing this through one Big Data system, you just won't find out the difference for a couple of years but, by then it will be too late.

So why do so many companies fall for this? What makes them think it is a good idea? Again, let's put this in estate agency terms. To put yourself in the shoes of a business owner that could get drawn into the idea that one of these 'open systems' or 'API' based systems was a good idea, we need to try to imagine we have gone back in time.

You have one of the traditional small data systems, which were originally built Before Big Data (BBD). As time has evolved, email marketing arrives. The estate agency software doesn't do it, so, begrudgingly you ignore that form of marketing.

Gradually email marketing grows and then suddenly you see the stats that say: 50% of people check their email account more than 10 times a day, and that it is by far their most preferred way of receiving updates from brands and you think, 'Ok, better find another system to do that email marketing'.

Now you are running two systems and the data is not connected, but at least the marketing is being done. Then social media marketing arrives. The estate agency software doesn't do it, so begrudgingly you ignore that form of marketing.

Gradually social media marketing grows and then suddenly you see the stat that **In 2015 Facebook influenced 52 per cent of consumers' online and offline purchases, up from 36 per cent in 2014** and you think, 'Ok, better find another system to do that social marketing'.

Now you are running three systems and the data is not connected, but at least the marketing is being done. Lead generation through landing pages such as instant valuations, ebooks and other downloads arrives. The estate agency software doesn't do it so, begrudgingly you ignore that form of marketing.

Gradually the evidence behind this form of marketing grows and you invest in some more systems. Now you are running 6, 7, 8 or more systems. The data is not connected and you are overwhelmed by the number of marketing tasks that now need to be completed. So much so that you even employ someone to try and stay on top of all this stuff that now needs to be done.

This goes on and on, with new flash tools appearing weekly from managing portal enquiries, email nurturing, sending out web based proposals, live chat, instant messaging, the list goes on.

Suddenly this feels very similar to the boxes of archived data in the basement that no one can stay on top of and no one remembers what information is inside them.

We have the data but if it got wiped tomorrow, we would not miss 90% of it, as we don't even know it is there and even if we know it is there, we are not using it for future decisions. We are just on the hamster wheel, trying to cover all bases with our marketing.

Eventually the small data estate agency software business providers realise this is a big problem and they make 'connectors' to each of these systems for you and this sounds fantastic! Won't it be great that your contacts will just appear in all of your other systems without you having to put them in there? You could even setup workflows in an if-this-then-that type way. For instance, if one of my contacts has had a valuation but has not yet instructed us, tell my email system to send them some nice emails about us. Sounds terrific! Sounds just like what you need. But it isn't.

There are a number of reasons why, over time, we have come to realise this is not the answer and will actually lead to an even bigger mess. The first is that if you recall from the last chapter, Big Data is about pulling lots of sources of data together in order to see and predict trends, give you insights and think up new ways of working smarter. With an open API system, there is no central source of data. The estate agency softwares are claiming to be your one central source of data, but they are still only working from the small data. The transactional data that you are entering. From that they are making 'other functions' work, but there is not enough data flowing back for the system to get smarter.

The other and, potentially more dangerous problem, is that this approach becomes unmanageable very quickly and, before you know it, you have created a whole pile of connectors, connections and triggers that you can't remember and can't check are working.

It was easy to set up a trigger to send a welcome email when you first started out, but 5 years later and with connections all over the place to do different things, will you even remember you have that welcome email set up? Have the staff changed since then? Does anyone even know it is still happening? Does it now say something out of date about your business? Has the logo changed? Probably the answer will be yes to at least one of those things, but remember there is no central place to update this.

The third problem is that at any point, any of the 100s of tools that you have connected up to could do some form of update, making the whole thing stop working as you had intended, without you even realising it.

The great Steve Jobs, Founder of Apple, explained this best when Android claimed that Apple had a closed system whereas theirs was open...

Steve Jobs... "Google loves to characterise Android as open, and iOS and iPhone as closed, we find this a bit disingenuous and clouding the real difference between our two approaches. The first thing most of us think about when we hear the word open, is Windows, which is available on a variety of devices. Unlike Windows, however, where most pc's have the same user interface and run the same app, Android is very fragmented. Many Android OEMs, including the two largest, HTC and Motorola install proprietary user interfaces to differentiate themselves from the commodity Android experience. The users will have to figure it all out. Compare this with iPhone, where every handset works the same.

Twitter client, Twitter Deck, recently launched their app for Android. They reported that they had to contend with more than 100 different versions of Android software on 244 different handsets. The multiple hardware and software iterations present developers with a daunting challenge. Many Android apps work only on selected Android handsets running selected Android versions. This is for handsets that have been shipped less than 12 months ago. Compare this with iPhone, where there are two versions of the software, the current and the most recent predecessor to test against.

In addition to Google's own app marketplace, Amazon, Verizon and Vodafone have all announced that they are creating their own app stores for Android. So there will be at least four app stores on Android, which customers must search among to find the app they want and developers will need to work with, to distribute their apps and get paid. This is going to be a mess for both users and developers. Contrast this with Apple's integrated App Store, which offers users the easiest-to-use largest app store in the world, preloaded on every iPhone. Apple's App Store has over three times as many apps as Google's marketplace and offers developers' one-stop shopping to get their apps to market easily and to get paid. swiftly.

Even if Google were right, and the real issue is closed versus open, it is worthwhile to remember that open systems don't always win. Take Microsoft's PlaysForSure music strategy, which uses the PC model (which Android uses as well), of separating the software components from the hardware components. Even Microsoft finally abandoned this open strategy in favour of copying Apple's integrated approach with their Zoom Player, unfortunately leaving their OEMs empty-handed in the process. Google flirted with this integrated approach with their Nexus One phone.

In reality, we think the open versus closed argument is just a smokescreen to try and hide the real issue, which is, what's best for the customer, fragmented versus integrated? We think Android is very, very fragmented and becoming more so by the day, whereas, Apple provides theirs with the integrated model so that the user isn't forced to be the systems integrator.

We see tremendous value in having Apple, rather than our users, be the system's integrator. We think this is a huge strength of our approach compared to Google's. When selling to users who want their devices to just work, we believe Integrated will triumph Fragmented every time. We also think our developers can be more innovative if they can target a singular platform rather than a hundred variants.

They can put their time into innovative new features rather than testing on hundreds of different handsets.

So, we are very committed to the integrated approach, no matter how many times Google tries to characterise it as closed, and we are confident that it will triumph over Google's fragmented approach, no matter how many times Google tries to characterise it as open."

Whilst I have not been talking about mobile phones, this damning speech from Jobs around the fact that as much as companies try to convince you that their platforms are 'open' they are, in fact, leading you only further towards fragmentation, articulates the problem very well from, possibly, the most legendary innovator of our time.

Who better to take advice from about the future path of your company than Jobs himself?

Chapter 5

It is a big decision, but it is now or never

The first few chapters of this book should have started to give you some idea of - What a big data system is and how it differs from the idea of just having big amounts of data and: How companies that built their systems BBD (Before Big Data) cannot help with this problem and may just try to muddle your thinking on the subject in order to stay in business.

Now that we understand this, I'd like you to start to think of setting up your own Big Data system like a bakery. A strange analogy but hopefully it will make sense as you read through this chapter.

At your bakery, you have the choice of buying in your muffins, pre-made, to sell them on at a profit, or buying the ingredients and baking them for yourselves.

The difference here is that the first option only allows you to sell muffins, you can't melt those muffins down and use the ingredients to make something else and you can't add other ingredients to them once they are delivered.

Whereas, if you actually have the ingredients, you can make other items with those same ingredients or even alter the recipe slightly.

When choosing to go down the big data route. The data that comes in makes up all of the ingredients that we have in the stock room in order to make our products, as opposed to a bakery that buys in their products.

This is a very important distinction to make.

We can use these ingredients to make ANY products. Whereas, businesses BBD are just bringing you one specific product that is very difficult to change.

With Big Data, you can add to your ingredients cupboard at any point by finding a new data source, such as how long someone has lived in the property, and then once you have that new data (ingredients) arriving, you can create the new end product from it, such as notify me when a property on land registry hits a certain length of ownership.

In this chapter, I want to start to look at some real life examples to explain how this works, in order to make this even clearer in your mind as to how that may work in your business. The difference between what you perceive to just be a useful function and how, when used correctly, it is actually just part of a Big Data play.

The first example I would like to explain is one that I regularly tell my clients.

Imagine a traditional High Street, in any town in the country. On that High Street, imagine that there is an independent coffee shop, where they make great coffee and do their very best to look after their customers.

The business is owned by Steve. Steve is a local guy who lives for his family and business. Steve has had his business for 10 years, recently celebrating their 10th anniversary and they have worked hard over the years to make sure they have all of their internal systems in place.

One day, a Starbucks opens up in the town. It does worry Steve, but he maintains that they are more of a personal service and that their customers will not only dislike the corporate style of Starbucks, but that they won't pay their prices either. Steve does, however, decide to go and try out the Starbucks, to see if there is anything that he should be changing at his business in order to stay at the top of his game and make sure he does not slip behind.

Steve finds the coffee average and the service efficient, but not personal and whilst there, he sees a sign to say that if you download their app, you can order ahead and beat the queue. Steve has his Skinny Latte, thinks it is quite nice and goes back to his shop. When his team ask him if he has seen anything that he thinks they should do differently, his mind is drawn to the order ahead and beat the queue idea.

As Steve thinks about the fact that we live in a world of convenience, but he also worries that his customers are more interested in the personal service, he wonders would they want to buy and run? Also if they did, would he begin to lose that personal connection?

Whilst considering it for a few months, Steve does start to notice a slight drop in revenue. He keeps this to himself, but wonders if the beat the queue app might be the reason, as there were no other obvious benefits when he visited the store. Steve and his team talk about how they could setup something similar, and one of the team is quite young and good with 'web stuff' so he sets them up with a landing page and they have a sign designed, similar to the Starbucks one saying 'Visit our webpage to order ahead and beat the queue'.

The page looks great. It has a place to enter your name, the time you want to pick up, and a text box for you to write out the details of exactly what you would like to order. Once completed, the shop receives an email with all of the information, so they can get to work on these orders and Steve feels quite pleased with himself that they are now on an even playing field again with the competition.

Now, let's stop for a minute and think about some of the things we have already considered in the first few chapters. Remember, Big Data is not about 'doing things', it is about gathering meaningful information that can help us work smarter.

Steve, the owner of the independent coffee shop, has fallen into the trap that most businesses make. He has tried to find a way to replicate the end experience, the part he can 'see'. So he has made what he considers to be the same function as Starbucks.

But, Starbucks ARE aware of Big Data. The order ahead function, whilst a useful addition and experience for their customers, is just an extra useful data gathering source for their Big Data. Starbucks had thought about the data they wanted to capture, and THEN came up with the app idea, in order to gather it.

When a customer decides to order ahead, they create an account. This information goes into their Big Data system and looks to see if the contact already exists in some way, but not just from being a previous customer. Perhaps they have just 'visited' the Starbucks website previously. Remember, ALL data is together in one system, even web visits.

Once the system has either merged their profile or created a new one and joined up all of the current information, it knows about them, i.e. what they have previously ordered, what they have investigated on the website, how often they have visited, etc. It will get to work, finding them through the marketing channels that are connected to their Big Data system, for instance, finding them in Facebook or getting them lined up to receive email marketing.

The client receives an introductory offer – order your first coffee through the app for free! So they do. Their order info now falls into the data: what they like, when they like to drink it, how much they spend, etc.

Using this information, Starbucks can start to work out when it would be a good time to show marketing messages to this particular person via email, social and even in print.

They can also start trying to figure out how to increase the spend of that person over time, by sending an offer on a larger size drink or a free cookie. Free cookies turn into paid cookies!

Remember, Starbucks are not having to look at individual people and make these decisions to send emails or other forms of marketing; the Big Data system is just doing it all for them.

Now, fast forward in time. Starbucks have been running that system in the town for 3 years. As each year passes life is becoming more and more difficult for Steve, the independent coffee shop, and he can't figure out why! He has even gone to the trouble of having an app built as he thought it was the same.

Because he tried out the Starbucks app, he has seen social and email marketing messages from them and so he has run random Facebook adverts, as he thought it was the same. He has invested in an email marketing platform, sent out leaflets - he just can't figure out why more and more people are going to Starbucks! He now seems to find himself spending more time trying to do marketing and run his IT, than he does in the coffee shop.

Eventually, as a last resort, he drops his prices, but that does not help either. He has a mostly empty shop, selling cheap coffee. He makes less money and therefore has to lay off staff, making the customer experience worse and eventually his business closes down. He never truly knows why it never worked out, just assumes that peoples' requirements changed.

As you can see from that example, Starbucks created a new resource of ingredients for their Big Data system, such as all of the orders, the type of orders, what up-sells work best, what orders go together and who buys what, when. It churned them around and then spat out better marketing as a product of those new ingredients. It was not even a fair fight. Steve did actually have all of the data too, flowing through his business, he just was not making any use of it.

Let's look at another example. The powerhouse that is McDonalds. They sell burgers, right? We looked previously at how they will use Big Data in their Drive thru, but what about inside their restaurants too?

If you are old enough, you will remember ordering your food at McDonalds and then keeping an eye on the metal shoots that the freshly wrapped food made its way down, in order to get from the kitchen to the server. Those shoots would hold columns of different types of burgers, all under heat lamps to keep them warm until the server needed them.

But around 2016, McDonalds started to introduce self service touchscreens into their restaurants. From the outside, this just seemed to be a natural progression for them to reduce staff, but actually it made their job slightly more difficult.

The reason it became more difficult is that McDonalds were trying out an idea. Was it possible to prepare EVERY order on the fly as it was ordered? The shoots would no longer work, as via the touch screens, people could customise their burgers, with either more or less cheese, none or extra onions, etc.

So this was an experiment for them, could they prepare food instantly upon order and still deliver it in the timescale people had become accustomed to at McDonalds?

With some trial and error, the answer was yes, but how does that help with Big Data? Well, aside from the fact that they are now able to analyse exactly what sort of common customisations people make to their burgers, and possibly stop spending millions of pounds on gherkins, the next step for McDonalds was/is (depending on when you are reading this book!) to allow you to download their app and - guess what? Order ahead! From the Starbucks example, we already know why they would want to do that.

Think about this for a minute. Think about the hoops, McDonalds have had to go through in order to prepare for and then pull this off, and now think about Burger King. It is not even on their radar (as I write this). They have not even tried to start figuring this out and, as such, watch as their custom begins to dry up and eventually disappear completely.

I recently visited a service station alongside a motorway and the KFC had a self-service screen, but I noticed that I could not customise anything. Have they fallen into the trap of just thinking McDonalds have screens for convenience and so we need them too? Will Burger King do the same?

Now let's look at Estate Agency. The small data systems that Estate Agents use are now beginning to allow you to connect up to external tools, but we already know this leads to even more confusion. As Steve Jobs said "you become the integrator".

The data that is already flowing through an Estate Agency is an absolute sea of ingredients to create some incredible products, but none of it is being captured. The industry just keeps looking for new one-off products to buy into and are ignoring the Big Data play.

They are offered new types of muffins to sell that will have a better mark up (get them more instructions or sales) and love the idea of the short term gain in revenue, but are not seeing the long term pain it will cause.

This leaves the entire industry very vulnerable, as one company could invest in Big Data system and only need a

The data that is already flowing through an Estate Agency is an absolute sea of ingredients to create some incredible products but none of it is being captured.

▶RS/0211 SEARCH...A01

TR/01▶03

▶SEARCH▶TR/01▶03

small amount of the national transactions in order to quickly move out of sight from the competition. Unfortunately, this story is happening all over the world. You might think, 'Wow, if only the companies had known' but from my experience, it rarely makes a difference.

'What?' I hear you say. 'If I had known this, I would have changed, surely anyone would?' Actually in truth, it is not that simple. It boils down to the same reason it is not that simple to change anything in your life.

The reason is that most businesses live reasonably close to the edge. Therefore, because of this, it is quite easy to sell products, systems and services to people that make them think they are going to make instant wins. It is because of this that the independent coffee shop owner was attracted to the instant win he saw in Starbucks. In his mind, order ahead = more orders. The reason most businesses do not make a change, even when they know this information, is that putting in place the systems to start building a Big Data driven company has no immediate payoff. In fact, it is just an extra expense.

So, for the same reason that it is easier to buy miracle instant weight loss tablets, than it is to face the hard truth that it will take some time to lose the weight which they have spent 10 years putting on, people procrastinate, without realising that literally every single millisecond they delay is critical and is no different to eating one more cake when you want to lose weight.

"It sounds really interesting and I can see this is the way forward, but we just need to think about it for a bit" is quite a common response and an understandable one, but only if you are not considering that this is, literally, a life or death situation for all existing businesses. If a business already has such a positive cashflow that investing in a new Big Data Lifecycle system is an easy monetary choice for them, they then also face the dilemma of: "Things are ok, why change them? Maybe I'll change when I see the rest of the industry changing." But the problem comes for these businesses at the speed of light. Some examples of this are:-

Blockbuster CEO Jim Keyes, speaking to the Motley Fool in 2008 "Neither RedBox nor Netflix are even on the radar screen in terms of competition,"

And here's Blockbuster spokesperson Karen Raskopf brushing off video on demand in 2002: "VOD is further off than we thought it was. We keep monitoring all this stuff and, when it looks like a sustainable profitable model, we can get into these things"

Sound familiar?

As I write this, Netflix is valued at $119 billion. Blockbuster filed for bankruptcy in 2010.

Nokia's Chief Strategy Officer, Anssi Vanjoki, about Apples iPhone: "Even with the Mac, Apple attracted a lot of attention at first, but they have remained a niche manufacturer. That will be their role in mobile phones as well." **At the time Nokia had just over 50% market share of the global phone market. As of today their market share is just above 1%.**

Porsche's CEO, Oliver Blume, said of Tesla's plans for the car market: "An iPhone belongs in your pocket, not on the road," **Tesla Outsold Porsche Globally In the 1st half of 2019 and, as I write this, Tesla is valued at $53.5 billion. Porsche is currently valued at $17.6 billion.**

The distribution and change that comes to these industries through Big Data and innovation is fast, it actually is life or death. For Estate Agency to survive this, you must be brave and have a very, very quick draw. There is literally no time to waste. It is now or never.

IT IS A BIG DECISION, BUT IT IS NOW OR NEVER

Chapter 6

It's not what you do, it's the way that you do it

Now that you have a good understanding of the importance of Big Data in the future of your business, and why you need all of the data points of your business flowing back into one central source, I would like to try and give you some simple examples of how businesses need to think about the ways in which they use their data, as it is not just enough to gather it.

As I mentioned earlier, the ultimate optional extra is the middleman in any deal and, all too often, the middleman ends up getting cut out of the deal once the other two parties realise that he or she is not having any significant impact on proceedings.

This is the wave that is currently sweeping through business. Companies that were built on the idea of being middlemen are dropping away like flies, as technology allows the original seller and the end buyer to connect via new distribution channels.

In one of my earlier chapters, I spoke about some of the most famous examples of once great companies that became middlemen because they let the data just flow through their fingers. Then, as competitors came into the market, they sneered at them, but although the new boy had far less transactions, they were working smarter with their data immediately. Let's just look at them a bit more closely to see just what a great height they fell from...

Thomas Cook: Thomas Cook was a travel operator listed on both the London Stock Exchange and the Frankfurt Stock Exchange. The Thomas Cook Group ceased trading on 23rd September 2019. Approximately 21,000 worldwide employees were left without jobs (including 9,000 UK staff), and 600,000 customers (150,000 from the UK) were left abroad, triggering the UK's largest peacetime repatriation.

Thomas cook were middlemen, sitting between the flight and hotel operators, and the consumer, looking for a holiday. This was an important service at one point in time, but technology such as Booking.com, Sky Scanner, and AirBnB made them middlemen. At their height, imagine just how much data they could have been using to create bullet proof walls around their business.

Blockbuster Video: Everyone knows the Blockbuster story. They were an American-based provider of home movie and video game rental services through either a video rental shop, DVD-by-mail, streaming, or video on demand. Blockbuster expanded internationally throughout the 1990s. At its peak, in November 2004, Blockbuster employed 84,300 people worldwide, including about 58,500 in the United States and about 25,800 in other countries. It had 9,094 stores in total, with more than 4,500 of these in the US.

Even though Blockbuster tried to evolve their service into a streaming service, they did not use their data wisely and, thus, allowed Netflix to walk into their industry without anywhere near the amount of Data, start to do much smarter things, attract more customers and give a better experience. They are a great example of just copying the functions, as they used the best developers they could find to recreate the Netflix website pixel for pixel, but were not aware of the data tracking functions going on under the skin, which could not be copied. Blockbuster became a middleman just focused on transactions, whilst Netflix were building algorithms and, in doing so, Blockbuster began to lose significant revenue during the 2000s, with the company filing for bankruptcy protection in 2010.

Phones4u: Phones 4u was a large independent mobile phone retailer in the United Kingdom. It was part of the 4u Group based in Newcastle-under-Lyme, Staffordshire. Opening in 1996, it expanded to over 600 stores. On 14th September 2014, EE and Vodafone, the company's final remaining suppliers, ended their contracts.

The company entered administration on 15th September 2014 with PricewaterhouseCoopers appointed as administrators.

Ironic that the development of mobile phones would destroy a mobile phone business but that is exactly what happened to Phones4u, as they did not make any use of their data, instead just focusing on how many transactions they could do and ultimately becoming irrelevant middlemen in the process of getting a new phone.

Clinton Cards: Clinton Cards was founded in 1968, when Don Lewin OBE opened his first shop in Epping, Essex. The business grew to 77 shops by 1988 and was then successfully floated on the London Stock Exchange. This enabled the company to increase its rate of growth and, by the summer of 1994, the business comprised 277 shops.

In October 1994, Clinton acquired 83 shops from Hallmark Cards and, in September 1995, acquired 112 shops from

Carlton Cards. In October 1998, the entire share capital of GSG Holdings Limited was purchased, adding a further 211 shops to the portfolio. These two important transactions and continuing organic growth were financed without recourse to shareholders. Who could have foreseen what was lying ahead?

In 2004, the company purchased the Birthdays chain of card and party shops, for £46.4million, but placed the subsidiary into administration in 2009, subsequently buying back 140 of the 332 stores.

In May 2012, the company's main supplier, American Greetings, bought £36 million of Clintons debt from its main lending banks and immediately called in the debt for payment. Clinton Cards was unable to make the payment and entered administration on 9th May. A week later 350 branches were closed, including all the Birthdays branches. The remaining 397 stores were purchased, in June 2012, by US based American Greetings' subsidiary, Lakeshore Lending Limited.

Clintons, as with the other businesses, had focused specifically on selling cards. The data flowing through their fingers was irrelevant. They had not looked to make life easier for people by remembering their important birthday cards for them, or any other form of innovation. They had just become a middle man that was no longer required, due to the ability for me to now order cards online and the services they offer.

All of these companies HAD the data flowing through their businesses, just as you do right now, but they failed to notice that business has moved on from just doing transactions, into one where the value of your company is around the use of the data you collect and how you then use that data to become uncatchable by the competition.

Think about all of the information that has flowed through your business in terms of the notes in your CRM. The data is useless now due to the format, but just imagine if it could be analysed. 10+ years of information about which sales go through and which don't. What are the commonalities there? 10+ years of information that shows how many times a person views a property on your website before they make an asking price offer, allowing you to be confident in your negotiation when their first offer is low? 10+ years of data on how long and how many touch points it takes for someone to become aware of your business and then go on to use your company to sell their home.

Automation to stay in touch with everyone forever; Automation to put the right content in front of the right types of people.

This list goes on and on and on.

Now imagine your competitor has this and you don't. Pretty unfair, right?

Not only that, someone can open up in your town tomorrow with a Big Data system and be in a stronger position than your 10 year old business within a month. Then, just like Steve the independent coffee shop owner, the writing is on the wall. Only you can stop that from happening to you, your family and your employees.

THE ESTATE AGENCY REVOLUTION

Chapter 7

Using Big Data to power up your revenue

This book is one based around the education of Big data and the difference between just transactional functions and building for the future, but in this chapter, I just want to touch on how having a Lifecycle approach to your marketing by using a Big Data system can have a direct affect on your revenue.

Market share. The obsession of an estate agent. Market share is something that is ingrained in us from the moment we enter the industry. I can remember as a junior negotiator, driving around the streets of Canning Town with a Dictaphone and a highlighter, recording the addresses of the properties for sale and sold, and marking off the streets I had covered. Of course, that was 25 years ago and there are easier ways of doing this now, by using technology. But my point is that the market share obsession runs from the very bottom of the company to the very top, but for very different reasons.

For instance, when I was a junior negotiator I was not interested in, nor did I understand, the profit and loss of the business. I was driven by the pure hunger to do my job well and prove myself.

As a more experienced Estate Agent, more market share in my mind equated to a more successful branch and more praise and commission. Actually, it was the praise and the recognition, more than the thought of the commission, as an extra few sales did not affect my pay that much.

If you are a business owner, it is all about revenue. Most small businesses live on the edge, floating between being comfortable and being uncomfortable cash flow wise, and over the years, I have learnt that the words, 'we would like more market share' from a business owner is just code for 'we would like to increase our revenue'.

The way most Estate Agents try to do this is by thinking of how they could either get called out to more valuations or to increase the amount of valuations they win and thus turn into instructions, right now.

Now, if you are a new start up or recognise that you are not in the top 3 or 4 estate agencies in your area, then looking to get called out on more valuations next month is a decent short-term strategy. However, when you do this you need to expect that your conversion rate will drop. Most Estate Agents do not have the means to track their valuation to instruction conversion rates accurately, so whatever you 'think' yours is, then 99% of the time it is incorrect.

At my company, Iceberg Digital, we have a Market Appraisals tool that agents all over the UK use, which has over £6 Billion of Valuations in it, so I am well placed to tell you that the average valuation to instruction conversion rate is around 30%. Now before you start celebrating because yours is 50% or 60% or even 80%., I must tell you that every single one of those agents that use that system would have said the same thing and some even still do, even though the facts say differently.

Even if your conversion rate IS 80%, that is unfortunately not a good sign either. That just means that you are not going out on enough valuations. Having a 30% ish conversion rate is not a bad thing. Actually, the general rules of thumb in business is that you should convert around one third of your pitches, one third will go elsewhere and the final third are still thinking about it.

As someone who has had the amazing opportunity to interview and work with some incredible investors and business people through my TV show and work, I can tell you now that, whilst you might be proud of your super high conversion rate, a conversion rate that is considerably different to this 33% rule, rings all sorts of alarm bells for a seasoned investor or entrepreneur.

So, as a business owner, once you are in the top 3 or 4 agents in your area, the focus on how to significantly increase your conversion rate on the valuations you go out on, is going to be a very difficult strategy to maintain. This will, most likely, result in your fees beginning to drop, in order to get more on, which is actually the opposite of the idea of 'we want to increase our revenue', because now you are just doing more work for less money.

So, where is this going wrong and how can an Estate Agency ACTUALLY increase their revenues, in the same way some of these incredible entrepreneurs and business people I mentioned would expect it to be done? And also, why the hell did no one teach us this BEFORE we started a business!!!

Let's look at this on a single branch level as some people reading this may only have one branch - some may have more, but if so, you can just multiply this up.

Stats vary from area to area but it seems that, as a ballpark figure, if you are up in the top 3 or 4 agents in your area, a branch should on average go out on about 40 valuations in a month. It doesn't really matter if you agree with that, or are thinking of a different number, you can just replace my numbers with your own. The principle of this will still work.

On the basis that 40 potential vendors have actually asked you to come out and value their property in a single month, and they did not just magically wake up that morning and think of the idea of selling and using your company, then it is reasonable to assume that much more than 40 vendors need to be 'considering' selling and using your services at any one time. Which is why you bother doing any form of marketing at all. In Estate Agency this is not really tracked at all but it is the **key** to increasing your revenue.

When you ask an Estate Agent about their 'conversion rate', it is universally accepted that you are referring to their valuation to instruction rate. There are no other conversion rates to discuss. This is wrong - very, very wrong and learning to monitor other conversion rates will change the way you run your business.

Actually, if you were to find yourself on The Apprentice, in front of Lord Sugar or a serious investor, some of the questions could get uncomfortably embarrassing for you (believe me I know, as I went through this uncomfortable moment with my own version of Lord Sugar many years ago).

So, here is the first question from Lord Sugar as you sit

in the chair, with all eyes on you... "You want my investment to help you grow your business. So, let me ask you this. The stage of someone inviting you to pitch to them (valuation), is called the stage of intent in the cycle towards them becoming a client. In order for you to get your 40 valuations each month that are at the stage of 'Intent', how many people do you require to be at the stage before that of 'consideration', in order for that number to be consistently hit?"

At this point, not wanting to look silly, you stumble and make up some sort of number off the top of your head. Lord Sugar looks a little perplexed, and says:

"Hmmmm, Ok, let's break it down further. There are loads of people out there that live in the areas you cover, who own a property and who may sell at some point in the future. How many of them do you need to be aware of your brand and have then moved on to the stage of being 'interested' in your brand, before they then hit the stage of 'consideration', and then ultimately the stage of 'intent', when they ask you round for a valuation? Further, how will you go about reaching those numbers consistently?"

You gulp.

That is the reality of business. Sounds complicated right? Actually, it is not that complicated. When you have systems in place to monitor those numbers, it is no more complicated that the fact that you already know how many valuations, instructions, exchanges etc. that you need to do. All you have to do is work on the numbers being correct by creating marketing for each of those stages listed above.

Let's try to make some sense of this from an Estate Agency perspective.

Luckily, there are companies out there that have already done the research to show how many people you need to make aware of your brand, in order to convert some of them into enquiries, or in our case, valuations.

Wordstream, analysed this over a period of 3 months, by looking at a wide range of websites and landing pages across multiple sectors, to compare traffic to actual conversions and found that 'average' sits at 2.35%. If you are over 5.31%, you are in the top 25% of companies, and the absolute elite companies out there have a traffic to enquiry rate of 11.45% or higher.

So, going on the basis of 'average', we would need around 1700 vendors to hit our website each month, in order for them eventually to begin to work their way down the process to get our 40 valuations. Of those 40 valuations, we can apply an industry average conversion rate of 33% that will go ahead with you within a few weeks, providing you have a decent pitch. So, 40 valuations will on average bring you 14 instructions, or at least 14 instructions that are not vastly overpriced or being under charged.

Now we go a little into the unknown, but let's say we sell 70% of everything we get instructed on, that would leave us with 10 sales per month. If we say that our average fee is £4000+VAT, that would equate to £40,000 of sales per month.

If we then say that 70% of all agreed sales will actually go on to exchange and complete, that would lead us to £28,000 of income from sales in a month.

Multiply this by 12 months and we have a sales turnover from one branch of £336,000.

Now, your average fee might be higher or lower, depending on where in the country you are based and your numbers may vary slightly. From this, you can see the principle, but what is my point?

My point is that the main number most Estate Agents are focusing on there, is the £28,000pm or the £336,000 per year and, whilst this number has obvious importance for you, this number cannot be increased, unless you start to focus on the other numbers. Each month the agents cross their fingers and hope that they will 'hit' these numbers. But they can't be sure, as they don't know the answers to Lord Sugar's questions above. They have recently sponsored a school fete or sent out some marketing and now they hope it will all come together, and often it does, but they don't/can't actually know for sure. However, it does not have to be this way. So what is the secret?

The secret is to structure your business generation around the other numbers we spoke about and employ systems that will let you see if you are hitting those numbers, in order to try and solve the problem BEFORE it starts, as by default we know that if we increase those numbers, the others will follow.

I call this, looking further down the funnel.

Let's look at those numbers again:-

1700 vendors hit the website in a month (or were made aware of your marketing somehow, via boards, leaflets, or whatever);

40 of them made their way from awareness, to interest, to consideration and finally, to intent and booked in for a valuation;

14 of them instructed you at £4000 fee;

10 of them sold = £40,000;

7 exchanged = £28,000.

Rather than ignoring that everything above sold, what if we place our average fee of £4000 against those other numbers too, to see where the money is leaking out?

For instance, although we were instructed on 14 properties and sold 10 of them, that still leaves 4 properties on the table, and at an average fee of £4000, that is an extra £16,000 per month that we are accepting will choose another agent, or are still just thinking about it, or are, as some may say 'timewasters'. But it is as we go up higher in the funnel that we start to really see how to improve the business.

The next level up says that we went out on 40 valuations and were instructed on 14 – that leaves 26 sales on the table. At an average fee of £4000, that is £104,000 PER MONTH who, for one reason or another, are not quite ready to instruct us just yet. Again, after a week or two of chasing, they are considered by most to be 'timewasters', but selling their property is clearly something they have on the horizon somewhere and, now that you have had the chance to meet with them and they have used your service for a valuation, they are effectively a client of yours. Therefore it is vital that you do not lose touch, with these people...ever.

Again, it is not feasible to think you'll talk to all of them via a diarised call back forever, but technology can take care of that, hence the reason there is £6 Billion of property in our Market Appraisal tool.

Now let's go up the funnel another level and say 1700 potential sellers had to become aware of you through your marketing, in order for you to book your 40 valuations. Again, using our made up average fee of £4000, that is £6.8 million of potential business PER MONTH that is fully aware of you, but for multiple reasons, not yet ready to contact you. This is such a critical stage of the funnel and one that many agents try for a bit, but then fail to see direct valuations from and so stop, or become inconsistent with it.

Using awesome content writers, or creating content yourselves, you can actually keep these areas of your funnel healthy, to make sure you get the longer-term benefit of turning those people into revenue. It is important for you to have a Lifecycle marketing system in place that allows you to see the great work they, or you, are doing is paying off in the funnel, as you will see the stages of Awareness, Interest and consideration expanding in numbers in your marketing funnel.

Now, based on all of that, what if you could increase the

numbers right through your funnel by just 1%?

Nothing crazy – none of this magic wand bullshit about how to become a millionaire in 3 months, just a simple 1% increase in the funnel. Here is what would happen (aside from Lord Sugar thinking you were the right person for him to invest in)...

You would attract 1717 vendors to the website instead of the 1700 previously.

Your conversion of them would increase from 2.35% to 3.35%, which would mean 58 valuations per month. Your conversion rate would increase from 33% to 34%, meaning you would be instructed on 20 properties per month instead of 14.

You would still sell 70% of them, as nothing we have done would change this, which would be 14 sales instead of 10. 70% of those would go on to exchange/complete, which would be 10 as opposed to 7, meaning your monthly income would be £40,000 as opposed to £28,000. This would increase your annual income from £336,000 to £480,000!

A whopping £144,000 increase from 1 branch, simply by employing marketing tactics based around a funnel – imagine what would happen if you moved from the industry average of 2.34% awareness, to conversion rate right up to the elite band of 11.34%??

Without wanting to bore you with the numbers, out of one branch, you would be generating £172k per month and have an annual turnover of £2m.

Now, aiming for the elite level might be a little ambitious and require a bigger marketing budget than is possible, but by using the same type of big data marketing systems that companies like Facebook, Google, Amazon and Apple use, and actually having the ability to see your funnel and strive towards a 1% increase is perfectly achievable, and let's face it, who wouldn't like a £144,000 bonus next year?

Chapter 8
The culture challenge

THE ESTATE AGENCY REVOLUTION

So, you have read the reasoning behind using a Big Data and machine learning type system to run your data through, as opposed to just storing it on a hard drive, and you buy into the idea. You have read about how it works and the fireworks are going off in your brain about just how transformational this could be for your business, and how you could take advantage of the data that already flows through your business. But I have some bad news. For at least 50% of you, the biggest challenge in moving your business to this type of model will not be a technical one, but a people one.

As a business owner, you are most likely to be either a visionary or an integrator. A visionary is the type of business owner that can see the future path of the business and has all of the ideas on how to get there, but usually struggles to actually get those ideas done by themselves, due to lack of focus. An integrator is someone who can get things done, but maybe sometimes struggles to think up ideas for the future path of the business. Whichever one you are, you need the other one in your business, or it will suffer.

In my business, I am the Visionary. I can dream up ideas all day long, but without Hayley, our COO and integrator, those ideas will just pile up on sheets of random paper on my desk, or stay inside my head. Hayley does not come up with the ideas, but she is incredible at getting stuff done. It is not that Hayley does not give the business valuable ideas, but they are usually around improving an existing product or service, as opposed to pushing the business in a totally new direction.

Now, when we go a level down from there, your are talking about your leadership team and staff. For a small to medium sized estate agency, you will probably find that your leadership team and the staff that carry out the day to day transactional tasks in the business, such as valuations and viewings etc., are pretty much the same people.

Either way, here is where your biggest challenge lies if you have bought into the idea. Depending on how long your company has been in business, you will have staff members that have a very specific way of working and have worked that way for a long time. Over the years they will possibly have heard some of your 'hair brained' ideas before too! You know the ones, it goes something like this:-

You walk into the office one morning and say: "Oh my god, I have had a great idea". You can't wait to get it off your chest and see the excitement that it will generate in everyone else! You proceed to explain your idea, badly, in the space of a couple of minutes.

One of the team you are explaining it to looks at you blankly. Someone tries to give a bit of encouragement by saying something positive, but it has landed like a lead balloon. You walk away frustrated and your team think you are slightly deranged.

As 'The Boss', you then take one of two routes. First choice is that you kind of move on from that idea and go back to doing some random work until you have another one, then repeat the process. The other common outcome would be that you don't let it drop and then force it upon the team and tell them this IS the way we are going to work.

Your staff will do their best to follow your instructions as you are the boss, but after a while, you start to find the new process is not really being followed properly, you get annoyed and wonder if you have the right people working for you. And that's the cycle.

This is one of the reasons that I said you will need to keep this book, in order to read it again, or refer back to it in the future when your team are giving you that feeling. To refocus and go again and remember why you are doing this. But there is a third option. I know as I have taken my own company through it, having suffered from the first two problems for many years. The third option is to start the process of changing the culture of the business. This sounds simple, again like you just tell people how it is now going to be and they do it or leave. Even though that is essentially correct, it is not quite as simple as that.

Before we can change the culture, we must first identify that we have a culture. Regardless of if you have preplanned that culture or not, you have one in your company. When I first started Iceberg Digital back in 2009, I did not understand this culture issue in the same way I do now. I did believe that we were creating a culture by having funky chairs, beanbags and a PlayStation in the office, but I was wrong. Those things do not create a culture, they just add to it. Let me try to break that down further.

The environment that I dreamed of in my head was one whereby the boundaries of work and play became blurred. An environment where people just work until the job is done, but equally, because of that, can stop and play the PlayStation, sit on a beanbag and watch something to make them laugh on YouTube, or read a book etc., whenever they want, regardless of if it is in the middle of the day. Providing, all the work gets done.

My problem was that I brought in the 'nice' bit, i.e. the beanbags and PlayStation, but without implementing any system for ensuring people knew what I had in mind. Therefore, when I look back, we initially had a team who just thought it was great that they could stop and play the PlayStation, but then they would bugger off home at 5:30pm and leave unfinished work on their desks.

I thought it was their fault and considered getting rid of the 'perks', but actually it was not their fault, as they had just never really been told the rules of the game. In truth I had not even figured them out myself, I was just frustrated that they hadn't been able to guess what I had in mind.

At the time if you had asked me if we had a good culture I would have said 'yes', but only because I did not know what a good culture actually looked like.

Back then, I would have said: "Yes, we have a good culture, we don't run a sweatshop. We give our staff nice benefits like a PlayStation in the office, free food and drink, etc". Now I realise this is bollocks. Don't get me wrong, we still have a PlayStation in the office and give the staff free food and drink, but that is not what creates a great culture. We just do that because it creates a nicer place to work. That is not culture.

So what is culture and how do you create and nurture the one you want?

Firstly, you must think about the type of people you want in your organisation. The most common mistake people make with this whenever I try to help a business owner, is that they start to list out things that every decent human should have. Things like:-

"I want trustworthy people";
"I want polite people";
"I want people who care"

The problem with phrases like this is that those are the things you currently hire and fire staff for, as you are not likely to continue to employ someone who is not trustworthy, polite or cares. You throw on top of this some targets and that currently makes up your hire, fire and promote process, right? This won't work.

Sadly, this won't work for your employees either, as they will just have a 'job'. One which they would happily consider trading in for another one if it meant even a fraction more money, for doing something they don't particularly want to do.

So how do you turn working at your company into someone's dream job? I mean let's face it, how many people truly dream of becoming an Estate Agent? Or an Administrator? Or a Salesman? Or a Programmer?

But here is the thing that I came to realise as I went

through this process some years ago. Actually there are not many people that do dream of any particular job - they dream of the things that go with it. For instance, when a child dreams of being an astronaut or a racing car driver, he or she is really dreaming about exploring or breaking records or being famous. When someone dreams of being a famous singer, they may well love singing, but it is entertaining people and the adulation that goes with it that they really dream of. Perhaps again, even the fame in some cases.

On this basis, what if someone who dreamed of being an explorer came to work for your company, because your business makes it a priority to be constantly exploring new ideas and concepts that are ground breaking in your sector? Or what if the person who dreamed of entertaining and gaining adulation is able to speak up on stage at your conferences, in front of hundreds of people and see their faces filled with amazement?

I am not implying that you should create these roles to keep your employees happy, far from it, but once you have identified what you and the company stand for, then you can start to try and identify the traits of the people who will LOVE working for you and those who work for you because they need 'a job'.

To do this, we need to identify what it means to work at your company. What makes up you as the founder, or the very best people in your organisation? Make a big list of the characteristics. Now that you have that, try to narrow the list down by removing anything that is something you would expect from anyone. For instance, trustworthy.

After that, look to see if any of the remaining traits could be combined into a different way of saying it and continue to combine or remove, until you end up with 3 to 5 specific traits that make up the founder and the ideal members of the team. It doesn't matter if none of your current staff have these traits, we are just thinking of this from an ideal point of view.

You now need to determine what each of these core values really means from the point of view of what you expect from the employee and what the employee can expect from you. You might even also be able to apply this to what type of clients you want to attract. For example, here are Iceberg Digital's core values and what they mean for our staff, plus what they mean for us as a business to our employees.

Be an Expert: This core value is around self development. We expect all of our team to constantly be self developing themselves, to improve the knowledge of how they work and their department, and even beyond that into their own personal lives. In return, as a company we are happy to buy our staff the books they want, pay for courses, let them attend workshops, walk out of the office in the middle of the day to listen to a podcast, etc. Just keep developing. What is not acceptable to us is for someone to tell us that they have been too busy to do any self development when it comes to quarterly appraisals.

Be Committed: This core value is quite self explanatory, but the idea is that whilst we have set hours of work, we have a team of people who just get stuff done. If something is on your radar, don't just leave it to someone else or leave it, full stop. Get stuff done! In return, we offer our staff unlimited paid holiday. We don't need to monitor it, take as much as you want, just get stuff done and be committed to the cause.

Be Connected: This core value is based around the idea that, as we all get immersed in our own jobs, we do not pay much attention to how the things we are doing are causing someone else's job to be harder than it should be. Therefore, take some time to stay connected with your team, have regular meetings, sit in their department for a day and just, generally, stay connected with the whole process of what they do. In return, they will want to stay connected with you personally in terms of what your goals and dreams are in life and see how they can help you move towards them.

Now that you have your 3 to 5 traits, these are known as the 'Core Values' of the business and from now on, you will hire, fire and promote based on these. In order to make sure that they don't just go up on a wall in the office and get ignored, you must create a structure around monitoring behaviour of these core values. The way to do this is laid out brilliantly in a book called 'Traction', by Gino Wickman.

Gino uses something called 'a people analyser'. The way this works is to list out your staff down the side of a page. Then across the top of the page, list out your core values. You can do this well in excel. From here, you mark each of your staff with either a + if you feel that they have that core value, a − if you feel that they do not have that core value, or a +/- if you feel they are kind of in between but not quite there with it.

The 3 core values at Iceberg Digital.

▶ **Be an expert**
▶ **Be committed**
▶ **Be connected**

You then hold quarterly meetings with the staff members individually, where you ask them to tell you how they are working in line with the core values and you also give your feedback. It is imperative that you do this every quarter and that they are taken seriously by you and your team.

But what the hell has this got to do with adopting a new software, I can hear you thinking? Well, having the right culture in your company makes these sorts of changes easier to implement, as you will end up with a group of like-minded people. You will no longer have people who look at you blankly when you tell them something amazing you have thought of, as everyone is on the same page and is a similar type of person. By similar type of person, I don't mean a robot army - I am a huge believer in a very diverse workforce, but I do also strongly believe that they must all have those same core values and believe that is the way they live their life. By having a team like that, you can have sensible conversations about why you are moving in this direction, or give them this book to read, knowing they will read it and come to the same conclusion as you, as opposed to having someone who doesn't want to read the book, ends up being forced to and then comes back and tells you it was a waste of their time.

It would be damaging to your business if you waited until you had the perfect culture before you made any of the changes required in terms of Big Data and Machine Learning, as it could take a while. But you should start moving towards trying to create the right environment for the type of people you want in your team to thrive and then start getting very picky about how the current staff act and the people you interview for new roles. If you keep doing that, it will naturally all fall into place and you will come to experience what I did, which was the incredible difference having like-minded people can make to your company. I now see this, along with the data in your Big Data system, as the biggest assets in any business. Regardless of if you follow the path of Big Data and Machine Learning, you should start to build your culture. It is just that it might be a short-lived success without Big Data.

THE ESTATE AGENCY REVOLUTION

Chapter 9
The Algorithm of Estate Agency

THE ESTATE AGENCY REVOLUTION

By now, hopefully you will agree with my claim at the start of the book, that I will explain to you in simple terms enough for you to understand the benefits of Big Data, the problems with older systems that just integrate with others and why all of this is critical to the survival of your business in the 2020s.

So what happens to Estate and Letting Agency in the 2020s?

It is a question I am asked a lot, whether that be on stage when speaking at events, or during interviews, or just in conversation with agents. As things currently stand, I see two paths emerging for this industry that I have spent most of my life in and love so much. The first is one that leads to a place in which Estate Agency, as we know it today, no longer exists in a few years time. Whilst this might seem far fetched, it is, actually inevitable if option 2 does not take place. I'll dive into option 2 further in a moment, but let's look at how I see option 1 playing out first.

The details of what I have laid out in this book come from my own personal journey of discovery and I am proud that so many people around the world consider me to be an expert on this subject. Having said that, it would be crazy to think that no one else is thinking about this currently. We have already looked at how companies like Google and Amazon are built around this kind of thinking, and how new super giant companies just like them are springing up every year.

Because very few Estate Agents, in relative terms to how many there are, have yet to embrace this technology, they are currently wide open as an industry to be disrupted using this method. A company such as Purplebricks, whilst struggling to be profitable and stuck at around 5% of the UK market share of transactions (whilst writing this book), still have more individual transactions flow through their hands than any other single Estate Agency in the UK. Therefore, if they were to start building a true Big Data system and apply machine learning to that system, they could start to become uncatchable as they begin to come up with the algorithm for a successful Estate Agency in the UK, that no one else has access to, thus increasing their market share and, in doing so, increasing their data, making the gap between them and any other competitor wider and wider and, eventually, insurmountable.

Another option would be for one of the current four horsemen of Amazon, Apple, Google or Facebook to step into the industry and do the same.

Yes, in the beginning their offering would be sneered at by traditional Estate Agents, just like Steve, the coffee shop owner, sneered at Starbucks in personal offering, but they would start to gain some traction, albeit small. Agents would continue to mock them, but as they did so, this new giant would be busy building their Big Data system until eventually they would be the competitor that you simply can't compete with.

As much as it pains me to say so, this is the path for Estate Agency in the 2020s. There is actually not even a small possibility that this won't happen to Estate Agency in the 2020s, as we have already watched it take place in almost ever other industry out there. Not the best news if you are running an Estate Agency... but... I did mention option 2. So how does that future play out?

Well, that one is brighter for Estate Agency, but it requires an almost universal u-turn on the way agents currently work. Certainly in the UK.

Currently in the UK most agents dislike one another with a vengeance. It is part of their nature. Almost as if they are at war. But from everything you have learnt in this book, hopefully you can see that unless we unite, no single agent has enough data to build the algorithm to save Estate Agency on their own. If you have one branch, a two branch firm can gather data faster than you, but the two branch firm will be outstripped by the 10 branch firm and so on.

Currently, at the top of that tree, is Purplebricks or a similar style company, who would still just lead to there being one mega company that killed all others.

Think about if we were able to unite as an industry, we could change the course of how this plays out. How? Because WE currently have all of the data, a central united Big Data system that agents use would allow the industry to become untouchable by these giant companies, but also maintain that your business had a competitive edge over new competition.

The way this would work is that the centralised system would look at overall trends and apply machine learning to them, in order to create new products and services to help the agents, whilst at a local level, the own agents system would adjust things based on just their own data, to apply the learning based on what their company data says. Yes, you would still need to go on valuations and explain why your

145

company is the one that the seller should use. Yes, you would still need to do marketing and content, but, you would still be in business. A very different kind of Estate Agency to the one we have been used to for the past 20 or 30 years in terms of the efficiencies, productivity and automation that Big Data Lifecycle systems would bring, but as an industry, we would no longer be open to disruption from a single source.

As the 2020s play out, it will be interesting to see the pull and push between these two paths. There are agents in the UK already involved in building both their own and a central Big Data system. Therefore, they will likely survive, but how many of them will there be? That is yet to be decided.

I can say from my own experience as CEO of Iceberg Digital, that more and more new start Estate Agents are investing in Big Data systems in relative terms to existing Estate Agents. Perhaps this is because existing agents have more upheaval and change required than someone starting afresh, but that argument could be countered with the fact that an existing business has a better cash flow to invest than a startup. Whatever the reason, the clock is ticking on Estate Agency as we know it. By building Iceberg Digital, I have gambled my future on the fact that, together, we can save this industry. Now, it is down to you.

Chapter 10
Closing thoughts

This was the opening paragraph of this book:-

The good news, if you are an Estate Agent or Realtor, is that this book was written for you. The bad news, if you are an Estate Agent or Realtor, is that you won't have a business in a few years.

In this book I will explain why that is in simple terms and also how you can stop that certain end happening to your business. I just ask one thing of you in return, you must finish the whole book.

Now that you have reached the final chapter, I hope that you feel that I made good on my promise to explain why Estate Agency is in such danger and, more importantly, how you can make a shift in your business to ensure that you are on the right side of the tidal wave coming in your direction. As I sit here thinking of the best parting thoughts that I can leave you with, I can't help but wonder about you as the reader.

For me, I am sat here now at my dining table, with a mug of green tea to the right of my MacBook and my phone to the left of it. I have word open and am typing away, thinking I hope this all makes sense, but I wonder about you; the reader, or listener (if you went for the audio book version).

I wonder if knowing this information will be enough for you? Could an Estate Agent or Realtor have managed to get through all of this book to this final section, learnt about the catastrophe of businesses and industries that never saw Big Data and machine learning coming their way and how it blew them apart, then learnt about how it could actually be avoided, and I wonder if, after all of that, will it be enough?

Enough to make you change direction? Enough to make you look at overhauling the entire way you work with your database? Enough to potentially make you want to convince your team that there is a different path you are now going to tread?   Or will this be classed as 'interesting' or even 'not that interesting' and lead to absolutely no action on your part?

I guess I will never know the answer to that question for every single reader or listener of this book, but I will put my contact details at the back of this book and you can find me on LinkedIn or Facebook and please, do drop me a message if you made it to this part of the book and let me know if it has enlightened you or changed your thinking. I guess even if you did not like the book, it would be good to know why, but mostly, only message me if you have good things to say, lol.

Writing a book is quite an enlightening process in itself. Daniel Priestley, who is a multiple best-selling author of business books once said to me that writing a book is great because it helps you, as the author, to crystallise many things that are inside your head and then get them into some sort of meaningful order, and he is right.

Estate Agency throughout the 2010s has been a carry over of Estate Agency in the 1990s, just with some minor parts of technology thrown in for good measure. Simple things that just could not be avoided, such as now emailing people information instead of sending details in the post. Using property portals and social media to advertise properties instead of the local newspaper and storing small data in basic computer systems, as opposed to applicant boxes and filing cabinets, but in the 2020s, it's time to actually evolve that industry or just stop.

We don't need to drag staff members kicking a screaming into the new age with us if they don't want to come. Generation Z is more than capable of stepping in for you.

When we reach the start of the next new decade, you will laugh at what Estate Agency looked like in 2019. This morning I visited one of my Estate Agency clients who after months, maybe even a couple of years of deliberation, has taken the bold step to move their offices from the High Street, to an out of town warehouse style office. Depending on when you are reading this, this may seem normal, but as of right now, this is very unusual.

Whilst I have been encouraging them to make this move for ages, I am not the one actually doing it, so all of their fears of being forgotten, losing business, losing face, being too far away etc., may well have been right. However, I am pleased to say that they are literally over the moon with the move. They are busier than ever, they have more members of the public visiting them than ever before, they have more space, the team love it and, through using Big Data systems and digital marketing, they are still reaching more people than any of their local competitors.

Why am I telling you this and what has this got to do with anything? My point is that the landscape of Estate Agency is changing. It is changing so rapidly that, if you are reading this book a few years after me sitting here writing it (Feb 2020), then I can imagine you may consider some of this information to just be obvious. For those of you reading this early enough for this not to just be the way it is, forget everything you know about High Street offices and small data systems with integrations. Stop and think of the new type of Estate Agency that will rule in the 2020s. What does it look like? Think about everything you have just learnt in this book.

Do you need to be on the High Street? Will that save me if I don't work smart with all of the data that comes through my business? Or could you just look to move to an incredible office space, with ample parking, that the staff love working from, regardless of its location?

What technology do you use in your everyday life that your clients should be able to interact with you from? Should they really **need** to come to your office for anything?

There is a serious danger in some industries that technology could replace the entire workforce. Whilst this is possible in Estate Agency, it is far less likely if we ourselves innovate the industry from within. Transform our businesses from being ones that are quite painful to work with, into ones where we do truly embrace technology. Where we do charge a fair fee for a great service that allows us to invest in the best tech, team and customer experience possible. An industry that could go from being ten years out of date, to leading the way in terms of how to combine the power of people and computers in order to find the balance required. An industry that could go from being one of the 3 most hated industries in the UK, to one of the most respected. An industry that could go from only being concerned about where the next deal is coming from, to one where the team are totally aware of their responsibilities in terms of data and customer experience.

Your business must be so much more than just a middleman that connects a buyer with a seller, since technology is replacing that super-fast, as you will know if you have ever bought anything from eBay or Amazon. Now I know that buying a property is very different to buying some pencils, but the idea that there needs to be a middleman for just that part, is a dying idea.

I have added some useful resources to the back of this book. Videos, score cards, articles, etc., that you should now go and work your way through, but before you do, remember, keep this book, refer back to parts of it when you are unsure. Read it again if you go off track, feel free to let other people in your organisation read it, but don't give it away. You will need it! Also, DO NOT forget, you are a data business. It is what gives you your advantage over the current and future competition. It is what protects from change. It is what will give you insights into things other companies can't see. It is what will allow you to develop an incredible customer experience. It is what will make you more profit. It is what will allow you to work smarter, and it is what will make your business very, very valuable, when or if you do come to exit.

The selling of a property is simply the tip of the Iceberg.

As a final request. If you have enjoyed this book or found it useful - regardless of if the book was given to you as a gift or if you bought it yourself - please leave an amazon review since this helps me to show its worth to people. It only takes a minute to do and authors like me depend on it but most people simply don't bother. If you liked the book and can do that 1 minute task for me, I would be very grateful.

Chapter 11

Resources

THE ESTATE AGENCY REVOLUTION

This is not so much a chapter but just a few useful places for you to now go to in order to continue your learning.

As of the time of writing (Feb 2020), these are all good resources for you to work your way through. Obviously, some may disappear off the Internet over time, or become less relevant, depending on how the world and Estate Agency moves on, but although many people don't believe me, I don't actually have a crystal ball!

So here is the useful stuff, which I may or may not have already mentioned during the book...

Raising Your Game: 'Raising your game' was a TV show for entrepreneurs and business owners. In the show, best-selling business author and CEO of Iceberg Digital, Mark Burgess, speaks to successful entrepreneurs to gather hints, tips and hacks that will help other entrepreneurs on their journey. There are 15 episodes in total, with some incredible gold in there. All episodes can be found on the Iceberg Digital YouTube channel.

The Innovative Estate Agent Facebook Group: A great place for agents to hang out and discuss innovation in their industry, as well as gain useful tips from others.

Estate Agency X: Estate Agency X is one of the industry's biggest learning events, where incredible speakers that are thought leaders in their fields come and talk to Estate Agents about how the rest of the business world is innovating, in order to generate ideas and inspire a better version of Estate Agency.

Blogs and Download guides: If you visit the Iceberg Digital website, www.iceberg-digital.co.uk, you will find hundreds of articles, videos and downloadable guides, all designed to help Estate Agents build better businesses.

RESOURCES

Printed in Great Britain
by Amazon